MARCO

SOUTH AFRICA

CW00327883

---

with Local Tips

*The author's special recommendations are
highlighted in yellow throughout this guide*

There are six symbols to help you find your way around this guide:

★

Marco Polo's top recommendations

sites with a scenic view

where the local people meet

where young people get together

(A 1) *map references*   **(0)** *outside area covered by map*

follow this route on the map for the best sights in the South Africa

MARCO ⊕ POLO

Other travel guides and language guides in this series:

Algarve • Amsterdam • Australia • Brittany • California
Costa Brava/Barcelona • Costa del Sol/Granada • Côte d'Azur • Crete
Cuba • Cyprus • Florence • Florida • Gran Canaria • Greek Islands
Ireland • Istanbul • Mallorca • Malta • New York • New Zealand
Normandy • Paris • Prague • Rhodes • Rome • Tenerife
Turkish Coast • Tuscany • Venice

French • German • Italian • Spanish

*Marco Polo would be very interested to hear your
comments and suggestions. Please write to:*

World Leisure Marketing Ltd
Marco Polo Guides
9 Downing Road, West Meadows
Derby DE21 6HA England

Cover photograph: Hout Bay, Cape Town (Pache/Erich Bach Superbild)
*Photographs: Johns (90); Kern (35, 37, 40, 42, 45, 58, 68, 88); Knipping (4);
Kress-Zorn (14, 17, 20, 22, 24); Lade: B & W (76), Dönit (65), Fiedler (11), Welsh (32, 61);
Mauritius: Gierth (72), Reisel (28, 31), Ricatto (66), Vidler (inside cover, 6, 9, 78, 84, 94);
Schapowalow: Moser (53); Schuster/Gössler (7, 62, 67, 82); Skupy (49);
Skupy & Hartl (30, 56); Transglobe: Layda (80), Richardson (26)*

1st English edition 1998
© *Mairs Geographischer Verlag, Ostfildern Germany*
Author: Dagmar Schumacher
Translation: Paul Fletcher
English edition: Cathy Muscat, Emma Kay
Editorial director: Ferdinand Ranft
Design and layout: Thienhaus/Wipperman
Printed in Italy

CONTENTS

Discover South Africa

A country of remarkable scenic diversity, from the red dunes of the Kalahari, to the dense forests of the Tsitsikamma mountains

The Republic of South Africa is a land of striking contrasts, a fascinating blend of modern cities and lonely Zulu kraals (villages), arid deserts and lush sub-tropical forests, vast barren plains and fertile swathes of land, high mountains and rolling green hills, with 52 nature and game reserves and 3000 km of magnificent coastline. Lying between two oceans, this sprawling country is five times the size of the United Kingdom, yet home to a population of only 41 million, as compared with the UK's 57 million.

South Africa was divided by the 1994 constitution into nine provinces: Northern Transvaal and Eastern Transvaal, Gauteng, North-West, Orange Free State, KwaZulu/Natal, Northern Cape, Western Cape and Eastern Cape. With its sunny, but temperate climate, the southern tip of the African continent makes an ideal destination for travellers at any time of the year. But for visitors from the northern hemisphere

Over 20 000 ships round the Cape of Good Hope every year

wishing to escape the winter chill, the best time to come here is between October and April when it is summer in the southern hemisphere.

South Africa has been inhabited for thousands of years, as evidenced by the thousands of ancient rock paintings scattered across the country. Bartholomeu Diaz, the Portuguese explorer, first discovered the Cape of Good Hope in 1488, but another 200 years elapsed before the first white settlers, led by Jan van Riebeeck, went ashore to establish a supply base for the Dutch East India Company. At the time of the Portuguese 'discovery', the Cape region was inhabited by the San, a nomadic tribe of hunter-gatherers, known to Europeans as Bushmen, and the Khoikhoi or Hottentots, who lived from cattle farming. In an attempt to encourage the new arrivals to put down roots in the outpost, the Dutch East India Company gave a reward to the first settlers who married Hottentot women.

To overcome the shortage of manpower, slaves from Malaya, political exiles from Batavia (present-day Jakarta) and blacks from north Africa were shipped to the emerging country. In 1688, the first contingent of French Huguenots joined the Boers, the name the first white settlers from Holland and Germany gave themselves. The French, forced out of their homeland because of their beliefs, were quick to identify the region's potential for wine production. But a visit to one of the present-day vineyards suggests that the German settlers also had an important influence on South African viticulture.

At the end of the 18th century, the British sought to gain control of this strategically vital settlement at the Cape and they finally succeeded in 1815 when the colony was ceded to the British. Under the new regime, the British granted 20 000 Hottentots the same rights as the 26 000 whites and they also liberated the 30 000 slaves, an action which was to have severe repercussions. This liberal policy did not meet with the approval of the Boers and many decided to head into terri-

tories to the north and north-east of the Cape colony. The 15 000 men, women and children who embarked on this venture became known as the *Voortrekkers*. The Great Trek, which started in 1835, involved convoys of ox-drawn wagons, which at night were arranged in defensive formations as protection against the marauding Zulu warriors. This was the second attempt to push into the interior. Some 100 years earlier, when settlers had sought to forge their way inland, they had been defeated by the formidable Xhosa tribesmen, but this time the Boers had superior fire-power. In one attack involving 12 000 Zulus, 3000 of the warriors died while the Boers suffered very few casualties.

The *Voortrekkers* established several territories of their own, which the British then seized. The discovery of large reserves of gold and diamonds in the north caused the disputes between the Boers and the British to escalate, culminating in the Boer War that broke out in 1899. Initially, the Boers gained the

Western Cape Province: the main wine-producing region

upper hand, but when reinforcements arrived from Britain the tide turned. The Boers, however, adopted successful guerrilla tactics and it took another two years before the British forces finally defeated them.

The conflict had a profound effect on white South African political attitudes, as the British forced the Boer republics to become Crown Colonies. At the end of May 1910, the constitution of the Union of South Africa came into being. Under the agreement, the four South African colonies amalgamated (the conquered Orange Free State, Transvaal, the Cape and Natal), and became one self-governing unit. South Africa's slide towards international exclusion began in 1948. The world looked on apprehensively as a policy of apartheid was introduced by the ruling National Party. This system of legalized racial separation was rigidly enforced by the ruling white minority. The government's legislative programme sought to slot everybody into a different racial group. It took over 40 years of violence and repression before apartheid finally began to disintegrate.

De Klerk, who won control of the South African government in 1989, decided on reform; in February 1990 he finally freed Nelson Mandela after a quarter of a century of incarceration, and work began on the negotiation of a new way forward for South Africa. In 1991 the apartheid laws were abolished, thereby paving the way for all the political parties to work together towards a peaceful handover of power to majority rule. In 1994 the first

The Basotho put their trust in the healing powers of the medicine women

free and democratic elections were held and Nelson Mandela was elected the first black President of South Africa. In 1996, the new constitution was adopted.

Nelson Mandela once described South Africa as the 'land of the rainbow', a poetic reference to its many different peoples and cultures. It is made up of the numerically dominant Zulu, Xhosa and Sotho tribes, smaller ethnic groups such as the Tswana, Ndebele or Bushmen, Coloureds, Afrikaners (Boers), people of British origin and immigrants from other European countries. There are 11 official languages, but English is spoken almost everywhere. Although relations between all these races are now much less strained, there is still considerable poverty and unemployment in South Africa, which seems all the more pronounced, as it exists alongside great wealth. On the way into the thriving city of Cape Town from the airport, for example, you will pass through endless shanty towns. To improve living conditions and build new housing would cost millions of

HISTORY AT A GLANCE

c. 1488
Diaz rounds the Cape of Good Hope

1652
First white settlers led by Jan van Riebeeck establish a supply base at the Cape

1658
Arrival of Malayan and West African slaves

1688
Arrival of the Huguenots

1779
First of the wars between settlers and Xhosa tribesmen

1795
English occupation of the Cape

1814
Boer rebellion against the British administration

1815
Shaka becomes king of the Zulus

1820
5000 British immigrants settle in Port Elizabeth

1834
Slavery abolished

1835
Start of the Great Trek

1838
Battles between Boers and Zulus

1859
Arrival of Indian workers in Natal

1867
The first diamond is found

1886
Discovery of gold. Johannesburg is founded

1902
End of the Boer War

1910
The British colonies and Boer republics combine to form the Union of South Africa

1948
National Party win election. Official start of apartheid policy

1960
Resistance to the Pass Laws leads to the massacre of 69 demonstrators at Sharpeville

1961
South Africa leaves the British Commonwealth

1976
Unrest in Soweto schools; police open fire on crowd of children

1979
First international sanctions imposed

1985
Relaxation of apartheid. Riots and unrest; proclamation of state of emergency. International sanctions intensified

1990
Nelson Mandela freed

1994
First, free democratic elections. Mandela becomes president

1996
Introduction of the new constitution

Johannesburg's skyline: the New York of Africa

rand. Such changes cannot happen overnight. The sheer size of the country does not make it an easy place to rule and unite.

The distance between Johannesburg and Cape Town (via the quickest route through Bloemfontein or the diamond capital of Kimberley) is about 1600 km. A large section of this long south-bound road cuts through the vast, arid semi-desert region of the Great Karoo basin. You can travel for hours across this featureless plain and never see another vehicle. Every so often you pass the isolated gateway of a huge sheep farm (some of which offer bed and breakfast at very reasonable prices), the only signs of civilization for miles. Eventually you come to the last mountain ridge that cuts the Cape off from the rest of South Africa. After a long journey through such desolate landscape, it is like arriving at the threshold of the Garden of Eden. Looking down towards the coast, vast acres of vineyards and fruit farms and, in the winter, lush green cereal crops, stretch as far as

the eye can see. In the distance at the foot of Table Mountain by the sea you may just glimpse Cape Town, known as the 'mother city'.

South Africa has two capitals. Parliament convenes in Cape Town for the first six months of the year and then, at the end of June, the government packs up and moves to the administrative capital of Pretoria. Cape Town lies on a peninsula with the Cape of Good Hope at its tip, the point where the Indian Ocean in the east and the Atlantic Ocean in the west converge.

The landscape of the rugged west coast is untamed and un-spoilt, as seen in the bird reserve by the Langebaan Lagoon. South Africa is unquestionably one of the top destinations for dedicated bird enthusiasts. Of the world's 27 different bird families, 22 are represented here. If you travel inland from the west coast, you will come to Namaqualand, an inhospitable and dry region for most of the year, except for the short period following the winter rainfall (mid-August to mid-September), when the arid landscape is transformed by millions of brightly coloured daisies, mesembryanthemums, aloes and lilies. South Africa's flora is rich and abundant. Among the best-known flowers of the country's 20 000 plant species are the national flower, the king protea, and the jacaranda tree (most beautiful in October, especially in the region around Pretoria) which bathes its surroundings in a pale lilac light.

If you are looking for a beach holiday, however, the upper west coast is not the place to go. Even on the hottest days the water temperature barely reaches 17°C. The best beaches are east of Cape Town along the southern coast and parts of the eastern coast. The fishing villages of Hermanus and Arniston on the Indian Ocean are the first places you'll come to with endless beaches. This is where the spectacular 225 km Garden Route begins, a wonderfully picturesque road that winds along the coast, overlooked for most of the way by mountains. During the spring, the roadway is transformed by extravagant displays of flowers in bloom. Resorts such as Knysna and Plettenberg Bay with its fine beaches, lagoons, lakes and river estuaries make this section of coast one of the most beautiful holiday areas in the world.

At the height of the season, hordes of watersports enthusiasts descend on the coast, but there is plenty to explore inland too. The forests here, the largest in South Africa, are home to herds of elephants. A little further inland is Oudtshoorn, the centre for ostrich breeding. If you visit one of the many farms, you can observe these huge birds at close quarters or even take a ride on one. Cango Caves, near Oudtshoorn, is a series of vast underground caverns, full of huge stalactite and stalagmite formations. Early Bushmen are thought to have dwelt in the cave opening, as stone tools and rock paintings were discovered here. Thousands of tourists now stream through the cave complex every month.

East London, at the mouth of the Buffalo River, is the only town in South Africa with its own river harbour. At the beginning of the last century, it served as the border town between the region occupied by white settlers and the homelands of the Xhosa tribes. Some of the places in the Transkei and the Ciskei homelands have German names, such as Hamburg, Berlin and Potsdam, as they were founded by German settlers who arrived here in 1857.

The weather in the province of KwaZulu/Natal, the Zulu kingdom, is frequently cited as the best in the country. Year round tropical sunshine and warm rains have created a lush evergreen landscape. The Zulus are the dominant ethnic group of this province. As a tribe, they occupy an important place in South African history. The greatest Zulu hero is Shaka (1787-1828), a fearless conqueror whose warriors were both admired and feared for their courage, determination and cruelty. A number of the famous Zulu battlefields in Zululand are open to visitors and well worth a visit.

The largest coastal town is Durban. It enjoys a sub-tropical climate which makes it perfect for sailing, swimming and surfing all year round. The people milling on the streets and beaches of this popular resort present a colourful mixture of western-style summer clothes, saris and Zulu costumes. Half of Durban's population is made up of South African Indians, the descendants of labourers who were brought to Natal to work on the sugar plantations. The few Victorian mansions that have survived bear witness to the vast wealth accumulated by the sugar barons.

Not far from the bustle of Durban lies the Valley of a Thousand Hills, a beautiful and peaceful region which offers some fantastic views of the surrounding countryside. Nearby Pietermaritzburg is a good departure point for excursions into the Drakensberg Mountains which encompass the Royal Natal National Park. Some-

The Berlin Falls in the Blyde River Canyon Nature Reserve

times described as the 'South African Alps', this range is dominated by the Mont aux Sources (3299 m). One of the most striking geographical features here is the Amphitheatre, a sheer 8 km-long mountain wall. Another main attraction is the many rocks and cave walls in the Giant's Castle Game Reserve that are decorated with San rock paintings. Country hotels abound throughout this mountainous region, which boasts some excellent walking and riding country.

The Orange Free State stands in marked contrast to the green and scenically varied landscapes of Natal. Like the northern provinces, the open country of the landlocked province only sees rain in the summer when the countryside is lush and green. In the winter, however, it is bleak, browny yellow, dry and dusty. Throughout the day, the sun beats down from a clear blue sky; in the evening, however, the temperature can drop from 20°C to below freezing within a very short time; suddenly the prospect of a night in by a cosy log fire seems very appealing. This rapid drop in temperature often takes visitors from the northern hemisphere by surprise. The main reason the nights here are so cold is because of the altitude; much of South Africa's interior lies between 1500 and 2000 m above sea level.

The two main conurbations in the north of the country are Johannesburg and Pretoria. They are very close to each other and yet in so many ways these two cities are worlds apart. Johannesburg, with its gleaming skyscrapers, is sometimes described as the New York of Africa. It is the industrial and commercial centre of South Africa. The Stock Exchange and most banks and insurance companies are based here, and English is the first language of most inhabitants. Known by black Africans as *E'Goli* – the city of gold – Johannesburg was, in fact, built with the proceeds of the gold-mining industry. During the 1970s, two thirds of South Africa's export revenue came from the sale of gold; now it has fallen to about 40%. It is here in Johannesburg that the differences between rich and poor are most keenly felt. The South African commercial power-base is surrounded by 'townships', home to the poor, black community. It is estimated that between 2 and 3 million people live in the 20 or so townships that make up Soweto (South Western Townships). Unemployment is high and the majority of people here live in poor conditions. In stark contrast to this, the northern suburbs of the city are inhabited by the very well-off, predominantly white population who live in huge walled villas, with gardens and swimming pools. It is not surprising, therefore, that violence and social integration problems are still rife.

Pretoria is a much more attractive city. It is the country's administrative capital and most of its inhabitants are civil servants. It lies about 400 m lower than Johannesburg at an altitude of 1500 m, and so enjoys hotter summers and milder winters. Further north, the landscape changes again. When the pioneering *Voortrekkers* arrived in the Transvaal after years of arduous travel, they thought the river that flowed northwards from it was the source of the Nile. That is how the tiny settlement of Nylstroom near Warmbad acquired its name. In this region of tea plantations and man-made forest, the climate is sub-tropical. Of the many waterfalls in the area, the Debegeni Falls are by far the most impressive.

In the north-eastern corner, on the border with Mozambique, lies the Kruger National Park, one of the biggest wildlife reserves in the world. Covering an area of over 21 000 sq km, it is bigger than Wales. It is not just the wealth of wild animals and birds that have made the Kruger famous, the landscape itself is simply breathtaking. The preservation of South Africa's wildlife heritage has a long history, with the first hunting laws being enacted in 1656. Founded in 1898 by Paul Kruger it was the first of many game parks to be established in South Africa. Golden Gate Highlands Park in the Orange Free State is another well-known reserve, where antelopes and birds thrive in a superb, unspoilt environment. Mountain Zebra National Park was set up to save the orange-muzzled Cape mountain zebra, slightly smaller than its more familiar black-and-white-striped cousin, from extinction. Lions roam freely in the Kalahari Gemsbok Park, and the semi-aquatic Tsitsikamma Park on the Garden Route is famous for its crocodiles and marine fauna and flora. Natal's Umfolozi Game Reserve won fame for its contribution in saving the white rhino from extinction.

Almost all the parks offer some sort of overnight accommodation, usually in 'camps'. For further information about the country's nature reserves, contact the *National Parks Board, Tel: 012/343 19 91*.

Most of the wildlife parks can be toured by car. In fact, the whole of South Africa is ideally suited to a driving holiday. In general the cost of car hire is slightly cheaper than in western Europe. The road network is good, on the whole, although decades of neglect in the homelands have left many surfaces there in a poor state, but efforts are being made to improve them. As in the UK, vehicles drive on the left-hand side of the road. Always abide by speed restrictions as the fines imposed for speeding are steep. In built-up areas, the limit is 60 km/h, on trunk roads 100 km/h and on motorways 120 km/h. If you prefer to let others do the driving, there are numerous coach tours to choose from. You can then benefit from the knowledge and advice of an expert travel guide. For further information, contact *Satour, Tel: 012/347 06 00, Fax: 012/45 48 89*.

South Africa offers tourist accommodation to meet all requirements and suit all budgets. The 1300 or so hotels range from one-star hotels which are of an acceptable standard, to five-star hotels which can compare with the best top-class establishments in the world. However, many people opt to stay in a guest-house or in bed and breakfast accommodation, as they are not only cheaper than hotels, but provide an opportunity for visitors to meet local people and experience something of the South African lifestyle (*Central Reservations: Tel: 011/880 3414, Fax: 788 48 02*).

South Africa can be roughly divided into two climate zones: the coastal belt and the Cape, and the interior. In Cape Town and its hinterland, summer days are usually dry and sunny. The hottest month is February, when temperatures average around 27°C, and the coolest month is July when it stays around a comfortable 15°C. Along the southern coast it can rain at any time of the year. The high inland plateau, the Natal uplands and the Lowveld in the north, experience wet summers. The rains, often in the form of late-afternoon showers or storms, fall from September to April. Johannesburg tends to be hottest in January (26°C) and coolest in July (17° C). The highest annual temperatures are usually recorded around Kimberley and Upington (33°C in January).

South Africa has plenty to offer tourists all year round. Game parks are best visited in January, when the grass is not very high. If you are not planning to stray too far from Cape Town, then the autumn months of March, April and May are ideal. The Garden Route is also very attractive at this time of year. As in all southern hemisphere countries, the peak summer season falls in December and January. During this period, many hotels, especially those by the coast, are full and the beaches are packed. So, if you want a hot Christmas, rather than a white one, you will have to book your accommodation well in advance.

'A world in one country' is South Africa's slogan. It may be well-worn, but these words are no exaggeration. Whatever time of year you decide to go, you won't be disappointed.

From Boers to Zulus

Following years of violent social unrest, South Africa's doors are now wide open to tourists drawn by its fascinating ethnic and cultural diversity

Afrikaners

The Boers or Afrikaners are the descendants of Dutch and German settlers, most of whom started their new life in southern Africa as farmers (*boer* is the Dutch word for 'farmer'). Their language is Afrikaans, a mixture of Dutch and German, but words from other languages, notably French, Malayan, Zulu and Hottentot, have crept in. The Afrikaners are very proud of their language, which is evident in the wealth of Afrikaans literature. Due largely to its Calvinist roots, this sector of the white community forms a very closeknit group. From 1948 to 1994 the country was governed by the National Party, the political party of the Afrikaners. It was responsible for introducing the system of apartheid, which eventually led to world-wide economic sanctions and a bloody rebellion among the black population. By the late 1980s, it was becoming clear that change could no longer be resisted. In 1990 the then pres-

Numbering over nine million, Zulus are South Africa's largest ethnic group

ident, F.W. de Klerk, grasped the mettle and set out on a path of reform. The National Party remained within Nelson Mandela's democratically elected government from 1994 to mid-1996 when the constitution set up a majority rule government.

ANC

Founded in 1912 and banned in 1960, the African National Congress fought a long, bloody and ultimately successful war of liberation against the white, ruling minority. The ANC is now the largest party in the country. Its leader, the Nobel Peace Prize winner, Nelson Mandela, became president in 1994.

Apartheid

Apartheid is an Afrikaans word meaning 'separateness'. Based on the premise that whites are superior to blacks, it allowed for the legal segregation of the population and the establishment of a social hierarchy according to skin colour. This racist policy was devised by the whites, mainly the Boers, to prevent the much larger black population from taking power. From 1948 onwards, a mass of racist laws were passed. The so-called 'homelands' were set up for the native black South Africans and the Pass Laws were enforced, bringing untold misery to the lives of the non-white population. Racial segregation was introduced into schools, hospitals and public amenities, in short all sectors of society were divided. The inevitable social unrest which ensued culminated in the Sharpeville massacre of 1960 when 69 peaceful demonstrators were shot dead, and the Soweto uprising of 1976 when the police opened fire on black children protesting against the introduction of Afrikaans as the language of instruction. Both these horrific events shocked the world. With the civil unrest and the imposition of international sanctions the apartheid system began to crumble and by 1990 had been all but abolished, though its effects will be felt for a long time to come.

Bushmen

Alongside the Hottentots, the Bushmen or San were the original inhabitants of South Africa. Small in stature, with some Asiatic features, they are easily distinguished. The few remaining members of this nomadic tribe continue to live very much as their ancestors did thousands of years ago. They live communally in temporary shelters, mostly in huts built from brush and sticks piled above small hollows in the sand. The Bushmen are a shy and freedom-loving race, who were forced to withdraw into the less fertile parts of southern Africa when powerful new arrivals began to claim the more productive land for themselves. The Bushmen have demonstrated remarkable skills for adapting to, and surviving, the harsh environment. The amazing rock drawings which can be found throughout the country provide valuable insight into the history and traditions of these resourceful people.

Cape Coloureds

Once a pejorative term used only by white racists, the word 'Coloured' is now an accepted term used by all South Africans. Cape Coloureds are descended from the offspring of marriages between Europeans and Hottentots, Malayans, Bushmen and black women. They now make up about 10% of the population and live mostly in Cape Town and the nearby provinces. A large, open stretch of land in the middle of Cape Town is all that remains of District Six. Until the mid-1960s, this poor, but lively part of the city was home to the Coloured population; however, as a consequence of apartheid, all the buildings, with the exception of the churches, were flattened with bulldozers — Cape Town was to be a white city. The Coloureds have not forgotten or forgiven this action and even in the new South Africa, work on the reconstruction of the district has got off to a slow start.

Economy

South Africa is rich in underground deposits of gold and diamonds, among other minerals, and mining is the mainstay of the country's economy. It has been the world's largest supplier of gold since 1886 and, even though output is dropping, the country still meets over 50% of world requirements. Modern methods are used to extract the gold, which is mostly buried deep below the earth's surface. It is not found in nuggets, but in the form of a fine dust locked away in veins of solid rock. Some galleries run as deep as 4000 m. All the gold mines are currently owned by firms which are members of the Johannesburg Chamber of Mines.

South Africa is also a major supplier of diamonds. In fact, there are very few commercial minerals which are not found in South Africa. For example, in the market for vanadium, a toxic silvery-white metallic element used in steel alloys, South Africa has no competitors.

Agricultural products, such as wine, cereals, cattle and sheep, are not important export commodities, but remain vital as sources of employment. The agricultural sector keeps more people in work than the mining industry.

The seas around the Cape yield in the region of 1.2 million tonnes of fish every year, about 90% of which is exported. Much of the crayfish served in upmarket hotels and high-class restaurants throughout the world is caught by South African fishermen.

Tourism is most certainly a new industry, but it has already developed into the third-highest earner of foreign currency. Now that the effects of apartheid are fading, the government is hoping to see an even more rapid growth in this sector. Visitors are clearly attracted by the sightseeing and the favourable exchange rate, and future prospects for tourism are

The protea, South Africa's national flower

bright as the tourist infrastructure is currently benefiting from new investment.

Flora and fauna

Few other countries in the world can boast such an abundance of plant species. This great diversity is due to the varying climatic conditions and the range of topographical features from semi-arid deserts to mountain ranges, evergreen forests to high grassy plains. Even the national flower, the protea, has 400 different species. The best place to appreciate the beauty and sheer variety of South Africa's plant life is in one of the many botanical gardens, while the nature reserves often provide an opportunity to observe both plant and animal life.

Most of South Africa's big game animals now live within the boundaries of the National Parks. Here you will see elephants, antelopes, lions, leopards and cheetahs, giraffes, zebras, hippos and rhinos. Monkeys and baboons also thrive in the mountainous regions. Of the 800 or so different bird species found in South Africa, more than half can be seen in the Kruger National Park. This is an ornithologist's paradise, but even the casual observer will be amazed at how many forms of bird-life there are here.

Homelands

The so-called 'homelands' were established by the National Party government as the cornerstone of its apartheid policy. The idea was to create ten supposedly independent states for the black population, leaving the rest of the country exclusively for the whites. The homelands were set up in the traditional black settlement areas; so the Xhosas were allocated the Ciskei and the Transkei, the Zulus KwaZulu, the Tswana Bophuthatswana and so on. These reserves, which only covered 13% of the total land mass, were home to 80% of the country's population and, as a consequence, became overcrowded and poverty-stricken. Most of the inhabitants were old people, women and children, as the family bread-winners were forced to work away from home, usually for the white community, in industry or agriculture. Families were torn apart, as the father came home perhaps once a year. Not surprisingly, these miserable conditions and restrictions of movement stoked up resentment that led to civil unrest. Now that apartheid has been dismantled, these areas have been re-integrated into South Africa, but it will be some time before the legacy of apartheid is completely erased.

Hottentots

Like the Bushmen, these cattle farmers and hunter-gatherers belonged to the Khoisan ethnic group whose history can be traced back 10 000 years. When Jan van Riebeeck landed at the Cape in 1652, the Khoisan tribes were widespread. Of medium build with light brown skin, they carried their belongings on their backs, not on their heads like the other black peoples of southern Africa. Sadly, the Hottentots are practically extinct, having been absorbed over the centuries by the many new arrivals to this part of the African continent. Some elements of their language, however, have survived in the Afrikaans language.

Indaba

Originally a gathering of Zulu chiefs, the term *Indaba* is now used to mean a political meeting or major gathering. The main tourist trade fair, for example, is called the Indaba.

Indians

According to most estimates, the Indians are the smallest ethnic group in South Africa. Their forefathers arrived in Natal in the middle of the 19th century to work on the sugar plantations. Most are Hindus or Muslims and they continue to live in Durban and KwaZulu/Natal. Like the blacks and Coloureds, they were seriously disadvantaged by the apartheid policy.

Inkatha

This political organization was founded in 1975 by the Zulu leader Chief Buthelezi. A rift grew between the Inkatha freedom party, which wanted a separate Zulu state, and the ANC who were fighting for one united South Africa. The differences intensified and the violent clashes which ensued put the 1994 election in jeopardy. Buthelezi and his followers were finally pacified when de Klerk and Mandela declared the Zulu kingdom an autonomous state. The Inkatha freedom party is now the third strongest party in Africa after the ANC and the National Party.

Nelson Mandela

After 28 years in prison, the 72-year-old Nelson Mandela was finally freed in 1990 when President F. W. de Klerk lifted the ban on the ANC. Initially sentenced to life imprisonment for treason, sabotage and spreading communist views, the former lawyer quickly became a world-wide symbol of resistance to white domination in South Africa. In 1991 the government repealed the last of the laws that formed the legal basis for apartheid. Mandela and de Klerk shared the 1993 Nobel Peace Prize for their efforts in establishing democracy and racial harmony in South Africa and in 1994 Mandela was elected the first black president in the country's first free and democratic elections. When Mandela was released from prison, the renowned South African writer, Breyten Breytenbach, wrote: 'He went in as an activist, he came out as a myth. Nelson Mandela is opening a door.'

Muti

Muti is the medicine (mostly herb-based) prescribed by the medicine men and women, and natural healers, known locally as sangomas. Mysterious shops in Pretoria and Johannesburg sell muti and give out medical advice. Sangomas are highly respected members of the black community; in fact, after visiting what we would consider a 'conventional' doctor, many people will also pay a visit to the medicine man or woman as a safeguard. There are over 5000 sangomas practising in Soweto alone.

National Party

Formed in 1912, the predominantly Afrikaans-speaking National Party governed South Africa continuously between 1948 and 1994. It was responsible for creating a very comfortable lifestyle for the white electorate, and incorporating the discriminatory and unjust policies of apartheid into the statute book. The grip of apartheid was at its most severe in the 1960s, when the Dutch-born 'Father of Apartheid', Hendrik Verwoerd, was Prime Minister until his murder in 1966.

Shebeens

Shebeens are the bars and clubs of the black townships. Originally, the term referred to the illegal watering holes used by blacks who were prohibited from drinking alcohol (the ban was only lifted in 1993). If you want to visit a shebeen, you should go in the company of a local guide.

Sport

South Africans are obsessed with sport. Cricket dominates the sports pages during the summer, and in winter it is rugby. There are no fewer than 400 golf courses and tourists are always welcome to play in return for a 'green fee'. Golf buggies are usually available and clubs can be hired at the larger golf courses. Walking and mountain climbing are popular pursuits in both the Drakensberg and Cedarberg Mountains. Bloemfontein is the country's gliding centre and, at the seaside resorts, you can choose between diving, sailing, deep-sea fishing, windsurfing and surfing. Many hotels have tennis courts and most have a swimming pool.

The population of Soweto is estimated at 2 to 3 million

Television

State-run television did not arrive until 1976. There are three national channels by SABC (South African Broadcasting Corporation) which broadcast in nine different languages, although programmes in English predominate. The privately owned TV company, M-Net, broadcasts films and sport in English. Most hotels have the special decoder, which is required for M-Net, as well as other better-quality video and satellite channels.

Townships

Early segregation policies introduced in the 1920s decreed that each residential area should only be inhabited by a specific racial group. Towns were sub-divided into white and black urban quarters, and in later years Coloured and Indian districts were also established. In the larger cities, however, the boundaries became rather blurred. Townships are, in effect, suburban ghettos. The term is now only applied to the huge settlements on the outskirts of the cities, populated exclusively by non-whites. Of all the townships Soweto, the South-West Townships of Johannesburg, is the best known.

These urban districts are in a state of continuing pressure, mainly because increasing numbers of people from the rural areas are piling into them in the hope of finding work in the cities. Less than half of all South Africans live in houses with solid foundations. The rest of the population struggle to put a roof over their heads with wood, plastic sheeting or corrugated metal. Those blacks who have got somewhere permanent to live, will usually rent out some of their space to those who are less fortunate. One small room in a hut is often used to provide shelter for up to 10 people. Almost 3 million blacks are undernourished, one third of which are children.

Wildlife parks

Visitors to South Africa who are interested in wildlife will almost certainly want to include a tour of at least one of the many wildlife reserves in their itinerary. Nowhere else in the world can boast such a wide variety of rare species. South Africa's 17 National Parks cover a total area of 3.2 million hectares. In addition to these, there are many protected reserves supported by the provincial governments, plus countless private game parks. Many of these are situated in the summer rain regions and, at that time of year, the tall, lush vegetation will provide cover for the animals. It is much easier to observe the wildlife during the dry winter months when the grasses are shorter. By far the best times of day are dawn and dusk. That is when the animals are at their most active. If you are planning to go on safari, then bear this fact in mind.

Xhosa

The Xhosa tribes, a Bantu-speaking people, had occupied the Transkei and Ciskei territories for hundreds of years before the arrival of European settlers. From the middle of the 16th century, the coastal communities came into contact with Portuguese traders at Delagoa Bay and shipwreck survivors returned home with tales of well-organized chiefdoms. A Portuguese journalist, who encountered the Xhosas in 1635, wrote: 'The men in this country are slim and upright, tall and good-looking. They can withstand hunger and cold and work hard. They live for 200 years, enjoy good health and keep all their teeth.' Today, the Xhosa population numbers over 7 million. If you travel through the homeland regions of the Eastern cape, you will see tribesmen and children ploughing the hillside fields with teams of oxen, while the women in their tribal costumes sit around smoking long-stemmed pipes. Their faces and those of their children are often painted with ochre, probably as a protection against the fierce sun. Xhosa women who have moved to the towns still follow their tribal traditions.

Zulus

The Zulu population numbers around nine million and forms the largest ethnic group in South Africa. Their tribal homeland is the kingdom of Zululand in Natal. They are renowned as fearless warriors and bloody feuds are still fought between members of the Inkatha, their political arm, and the governing ANC party. At the beginning of the last century, the Zulu warriors were greatly feared throughout the region. Their king, Shaka, was regarded as a military genius and legends of his violent exploits still circulate. His vast army consisted of 50 000 men and 10 000 women and his kingdom extended along the Tugela River, covering most of the Natal area. Shaka's reputation as a merciless leader is derived from tales of his military victories. When he defeated a tribe, it is said that he had all the chiefs, women and children murdered. But his thirst for blood and power led to his own death. He was murdered by his brother, Dingaan, who then seized control of the Zulu kingdom. Dingaan led the Zulu army against the Boers and later against the British colonial troops. In 1872, after the final, decisive battle in Ulundi, the victorious British divided the kingdom that Shaka had founded into 13 regions, each with its own chief.

Choice wines with ethnic specialities

South Africa's excellent wines complement any menu, whether Indian or Malayan, European or Afrikaans

Food

South African cuisine is more regional than national, offering a range of food that is as varied as the population is diverse. Though the predominant influences are either European or Asian, each region has developed its own unique specialities and you will experience many new and unusual tastes.

Around the Cape Town area, the cuisine is mainly Malayan influenced. Among the most popular dishes here are *bobotie*, an oven-baked curry made with minced lamb and potatoes, and *bredie*, a stew made from lamb or mutton and vegetables. Tomato *bredies* are particularly tasty. *Koeksisters* are popular sweets (also Malayan in origin). They are small pastries made of fruit and nuts which are fried then dipped in honey or syrup.

Given that half the population of Durban is of Indian and Asian origin, the cuisine of the Natal region naturally has a strong Indian influence. Local specialities

Sorghum beer, a refreshing home brew

include spicy fish or meat curries served with sweet and sour chutney, and samosas — crispy, triangular pastries with a spicy vegetable or meat filling.

Like the Australians, there is nothing South Africans love more than a good barbecue. Take a tour through the outskirts of any South African city on a summer weekend and the air will be filled with the mouthwatering smell of char-grilled meat. These *braai* parties, as they are called, are lively and informal occasions. People stand around the barbecue chatting and drinking beers while generous portions of meat are grilled over an open flame. The choice of meats on offer would typically include top-grade steaks, lamb and pork cuts, long sausages known as *boerewors*, and *sosaties* — kebabs made with chunks of lamb, dried fruits, apple rings and tomatoes. *Stywe pap* is the typical accompaniment to these barbecued meats (the sausages in particular). It is a type of porridge made from boiled cornflour which is shaped into a dumpling between the hands and then dipped into a sauce.

The majority of restaurants include a range of fish dishes on the menu. Fish is an especially good choice in the coastal regions, where it is almost certain to be fresh. Look out for crayfish, a delicacy that is considerably cheaper here than it is in Europe. Before you place your order, however, you should ask whether it is fresh, as frozen crayfish is nowhere near as tasty. *Kingklip* is a local fish much appreciated by South Africans. It has firm, white flesh and is usually served filleted and grilled. *Snoek* is another popular speciality. A rich and oily fish that looks like barracuda, it is usually served smoked and can be bought flavoured with herbs or whole peppercorns. *Perlemoen*, also known as abalone, is a large hand-sized shellfish, that thrives along the Atlantic shore.

A wide range of fruit and vegetables is available in the shops and markets, and is generally of very high quality. Thanks to the favourable climate, most of the produce can be grown outdoors, rather than in greenhouses, which invariably improves the aroma and flavour. Mushrooms are the only exception – they are as pale and insipid as those sold in the supermarkets back home. Most of the asparagus on sale in South Africa is green-stemmed. Farmers have only recently started to cultivate white asparagus. The dessert grapes, melons and apples cultivated here are definitely worth sampling.

Most of the fruit and vegetables on offer will be familiar, but you may come across one or two varieties you haven't seen before. Cape gooseberries, for example, are unique to the region around Cape Town. These large yellow berries are mainly used for making cakes and jams. One of the more unusual South African ingredients is *waterblommetjie*. Similar to the water lily, this flower can be seen growing on ponds in the Cape region from May onwards, and it is often added to lamb stews.

Biltong is another unique South African speciality. Although these strips of meat do not look partic-

The market stalls overflow with sweet and juicy fruit throughout the year

24

ularly appetizing they taste delicious. The meat is either beef, venison or ostrich, which is salted, spiced and air-dried. You will see it hanging behind the counter in specialist shops, butchers and supermarkets. A special machine is used to cut the dried meat into manageable pieces. Toothpicks are also supplied.

Drink

Tap water is safe to drink everywhere in South Africa; in fact, the country claims to have the purest drinking water in the world. Only in very recent years has mineral water become fashionable. In restaurants, South Africans often order a glass of iced water, mainly as a thirst quencher when temperatures rise. Among the black population, the most popular alcoholic beverage is beer, while white South Africans tend to drink more spirits. Brandy and coke is a favourite tipple. Gin, rum, vodka and whisky are usually served on the rocks with a variety of mixers. Many fruit brandies are produced or at least bottled in South Africa.

Although grapes have been grown in the country for over 300 years, the reputation South African wine now enjoys around the world has only been gained over the last 15 years. The area around Cape Town is a haven for winedrinkers. The properties of the soil and the sunny climate provide perfect conditions for the cultivation of vines. If you are starting your tour of South Africa at Cape Town, why not follow the wine routes from Franschhoek, Stellenbosch, Paarl or Constantia. You can stop off en route and sample some of the region's best table wines and then stock up for the rest of your journey. Among the best-known producers are: Meerlust (red wine); De Wetshof and Klein Constantia (white wine); the estates of Blaauwklippen, Boschendal, Le Bonheur, L'Ormarins, Nederburg, Rustenberg, Simonsig and Stellenryck (red and white wine).

South Africans tend to drink filter and instant coffee, though many restaurants serve espresso and cappuccino. *Rooibos* tea is worth sampling. A cross between herbal tea and black tea, it tastes strange at first, but you may find you acquire a taste for it. Made from the fine twigs and fruit of the 'red bush', which only grows in the area around Clanwilliam on the west coast, it is quite refreshing when chilled.

Restaurants

You will find a wide choice of restaurants in the major cities and resorts. All of South Africa's many different cuisines are usually represented on the menu. Some restaurants only have a license to sell beer and wine while others, particularly the smaller ones, are not licensed at all. If you go to an unlicensed restaurant, then you can take your own drinks with you and you will just be charged for corkage. Bottle stores are the local equivalent to off-licences. Supermarkets do not normally sell alcoholic drinks. When you book a table, you will usually be advised whether the restaurant is licensed or not. It is always worth taking the precaution of booking a table in the evenings, particularly in the main cities. Some restaurants and hotels may also insist on smart dress.

Diamonds and beads

All the arts and crafts reflect a distinctive regional or tribal style

Given its mixed ethnic composition and the sheer size of the country, it is not surprising that South Africa boasts such a rich heritage of traditional arts and crafts. You'll come across a wide variety of objects which all reflect a distinctive regional or tribal style: clothes and fabrics printed with African designs, jewellery, objets d'art such as wood-carvings, and a whole array of items made from beads. African beadwork is particularly fascinating as each carefully crafted piece carries its own message or symbol. Zulus and Xhosas, for example, send small carpets of beads which carry love messages in their patterns.

Each of the Bantu tribes have developed their own particular skills and specialities. Zulus make little dolls embroidered with beads, transform pine cones into birds and cover gourds with beads to make them into containers known as calabashes. Typical Xhosa crafts include the *inxhili*,

Bustling market in front of Cape Town town hall

a traditional white and orange bag decorated with beads and buttons, and *isibinquo*, an embroidered skirt with matching waistcoat. You will also find pretty tablecloths in the same designs. The long, bead-studded pipes are called *inquawe*.

The Ndebele are famous for their beaded goatskin loincloths, which are worn by both men and women and come in a variety of sizes. The bead embroidery on the woman's garment indicates whether she is married, and on a young man, whether he has undergone his manhood ritual. Their tall dolls (up to a metre in length), embroidered with beads, are symbols of fertility and masculinity. Ndebele brides wear a special headdress known as a *nyoka*. The beaded jewellery, bangles and necklaces are very colourful and, if the opportunity arises, it is fascinating to watch how they are made.

Many of these souvenirs can be bought on the streets and in the tourist shops. Most major towns have weekend flea markets where traders gather to sell their own handmade crafts. These will

The Ndebele are famous for their elaborate and colourful designs

usually have been produced in backstreet workshops in the black quarters.

You will often see children from the black townships standing on street corners selling handicrafts and toys, such as windmills, toy cars and bicycles imaginatively crafted from wire and tin, skills that have been acquired out of necessity.

If you are interested in antiques (mostly brought over from Europe by immigrants) and bric-à-brac, then you will probably find some good bargains here too. Cape Town and Johannesburg are the main centres for antiques.

Even though South Africa is renowned for its rich gold and diamond reserves, the cost of jewellery is not necessarily lower. The price of gold and precious stones here is still determined by the international market. How-ever, if you shop around you can pick up some good reasonably-priced pieces. An item of jewellery that is hand-made in South Africa, for example, will be cheaper because wage levels are much lower than in any western European country. The quality of the craftsmanship is usually superb, but make sure you buy from a 'master goldsmith'. The price of diamonds and other gems is comparatively reasonable, but they should only be purchased in specialist shops. If you buy imported jewellery, it will be subject to the import tax surcharge placed on luxury goods of 85%. VAT is payable on jewellery, but you can claim the money back at the airport on presentation of the item with the receipt and special form that should have been issued by the shop.

Ostriches are reared in South Africa both for their meat and the leather which is used to make purses, wallets, handbags, suitcases and even shoes. You should exercise caution, however, when buying goods made from animals, for both moral and legal reasons. Protected and endangered species such as elephants, snakes, leopards and turtles are still being illegally hunted for their tusks, skins and shells.

Shops are open *Monday to Friday* from *08.30-17.00, Saturday 08.30-13.00*. The corner shops and kiosks you will find in practically every town and village are misleadingly known as cafés. They sell soft drinks, newspapers, food, cigarettes, sweets, etc. and many also sell snacks and fast food too. They often open as early as 06.00 and don't usually close before midnight.

Carnivals, street fairs and festivals

*A colourful blend of folklore, garlands, music and dancing
make for some unforgettable experiences*

PUBLIC HOLIDAYS

1 January: *New Year's Day*
21 March: *Human Rights Day*
(commemoration of the Sharpeville massacre, 1960)
March/April: *Good Friday, Easter
Monday*
27 April: *Freedom Day* (commemoration of the first democratic
elections, 1994)
16 June: *Youth Day* (commemoration of the Soweto uprising, 1976)
9 August: *National Women's Day*
24 September: *Heritage Day*
16 December: *Day of Reconciliation*
25/26 December: *Christmas*
If one of these dates falls on a
Sunday, the following Monday is
a holiday.

RELIGIOUS HOLIDAYS

Around three quarters of all
South Africans are Christians, so
Christmas and Easter are holidays
throughout the country. Other
events in the Christian calendar
are celebrated by the various denominations. In Cape Town and
Johannesburg many businesses
are closed for the main Jewish
holidays. Most South Africans

of Malayan origin are Muslims,
while the Indians in Natal are
mainly Hindus: these communities have their own holidays.

FESTIVALS & LOCAL EVENTS

1-7 January

★ *Cape Town Carnival.* Lively
street carnival where groups of
people parade through the city
dressed in colourful costumes,
some playing music with stringed
instruments and saxophones and
others dancing. The highlight
is the competition held in Green
Point Stadium, where the best
band is chosen.
Information: Tel: 021/397 64 29

March

Last weekend in March: *Durban
Fiesta and Harbour Festival.* Town
and harbour festival in Durban,
ending with beach barbecues.

March/April

Rand Show in Johannesburg. One
of South Africa's top trade fairs.

31 May

Comrades Marathon. Annual race
from Pietermaritzburg to Durban.

29

Traditional tribal dances are often performed at local festivals

MARCO POLO SELECTION: EVENTS

1 Cape Town Carnival
The Cape Coloureds' music festival is one of the main highlights of the holiday season (page 29)

2 Steam Festival in Kimberley
The diamond town's impressive collection of old steam locomotives are cleaned up for this July festival (page 31)

June

Grahamstown Arts Festival. A 10-day cultural festival with a packed programme of film, theatre, music and dance events. *Information: Tel: 0461/271 15*

Mid-June: *Zululand Show.* Big Zulu show combined with an agricultural exhibition in Eshowe.

July

First weekend of July: *Durban July.* The highlight of the horse-racing season held at Greyville racetrack in Durban.

Third weekend of July: *Shembe festival.* Zulu religious festival with tribal dancing held in Eku-pakuneni near Durban.

Last weekend of July: ★ *Kimberley Steam Festival.* The town's full collection of steam locomotives is put on display.

October

Third week in October: *Bloemfontein Rose Festival.* A lovely flower festival which does justice to the city's name which literally means 'spring of flowers'.

Last Weds-Sat in October: *Stellenbosch Food and Wine Festival.* This event provides an opportunity to sample all the wines produced in the Stellenbosch region.

A Zulu in full regalia at a Durban festival

Jacaranda Carnival. When the jacaranda trees are in full bloom, Pretoria celebrates with a lively street festival.

Durban Tatoo. Fireworks and plenty of music.

December

1 Million Golf Tournament. Only the best players in the world are invited to compete in this prestigious event held at Sun City/Lost City.

Third week in December: ✦ *Rothmans Week.* This sailing regatta, from Cape Town to Saldanha, is the biggest and most elaborate sailing event held in South Africa.

At the tip of Africa

Cape Town lies within easy reach of flourishing vineyards, vast mountain ranges, barren deserts and attractive bays

The three Cape provinces, the Northern Cape, the Western Cape and the Eastern Cape, together make up 60% of the country's total land mass. Scenic contrasts are provided by the varied and stunning landscapes that range from stony deserts and mountain chains to wide floral belts and rolling vineyards.

An exploratory tour of the Cape Peninsula is definitely worthwhile. It is about 51 km long and no more than 16 km wide, and its hills overlook the oceans on both sides. Cape Town with its plush, exclusive suburbs and atmospheric old harbour, nestles in the lap of the flat-topped Table Mountain. Aside from the historic city there is still plenty to discover on the peninsula: small fishing villages, magnificent coast roads, superb beaches, nature reserves and, at the southernmost tip, the Cape of Good Hope, described by Sir Francis Drake as the 'prettiest cape that we saw anywhere in the world'.

Cape Town enjoys a spectacular setting at the foot of Table Mountain

Hotel and Restaurant Prices

Hotels
Category 1: over £35
Category 2: £27-£35
Category 3: below £27
(*Prices for a double room with breakfast*)

Restaurants
Category 1: over £17
Category 2: £10-£17
Category 3: below £10
(*Prices for one meal with starter, main course, dessert and drink*)

There is no shortage of hotels and guest houses in the main tourist areas, and most of the Nature Reserves offer accommodation in hutted camps. Given the increasing popularity of South Africa as a holiday destination, however, it is always best to book your accommodation well in advance, especially during peak season.

The northern suburbs of Cape Town mark the beginning of the wine-producing region where vineyards surround country residences built in characteristic Cape Dutch style. For over 300 years, this soil has yielded some outstanding vintages.

The Cape provinces include large sections of the Karoo. This is the perfect region for those in search of peace, seclusion and a classic African desert landscape. A remarkable atmosphere pervades the whole area, created by the combination of tranquillity, uninterrupted expanses of land and a unique quality of light. This vast semi-desert, dotted with small bushes, is home to thousands of sheep. At some point on your travels, you will have the opportunity to taste the distinctively flavoured meat from lambs reared on the Karoo plains.

The Indian Ocean side of the Cape is extraordinarily green and fertile. Water supply actually exceeds demand. The main attraction of this coastal stretch is the famous Garden Route. It is not, as the name suggests, a trail past a series of traditional gardens. It is, quite simply, a very attractive route through a beautiful untamed landscape. Not a European garden with neatly manicured lawns, but an African garden with a rugged coastline, sombre rainforests, sweeping beaches, rows of serrated mountain peaks and cosy hamlets nestling between sea and land. The best way to appreciate the contrasting landscapes is to approach the coastal region from the Karoo via the Swartberg Pass.

Probably the finest stretch of coast road lies between Mossel Bay and the mouth of the Storm

MARCO POLO SELECTION: THE CAPE PROVINCES

1 Table Mountain
Take a cable-car to the top of the 1000-m high mountain (page 37)

2 Cape of Good Hope
Spectacular panoramas out to sea and over the Cape peninsula (page 41)

3 Plettenberg Bay
Exclusive resort on the Garden Route (page 54)

4 Stellenbosch
South Africa's second oldest town lies at the centre of the wine-producing region (page 59)

5 Kirstenbosch Botanical Garden
The best time to visit this amazing botanical garden on the slopes of Table Mountain is in the spring, from August to October (page 37)

6 Kalahari Gemsbok Park
The unspoilt, semi-arid landscape of South Africa's second-largest reserve is teeming with wildlife (page 52)

7 Cango Caves
The fantastic stalactite and stalagmite caves near Oudtshoorn are unmissable (page 48)

Company's Garden is one of Cape Town's most popular parks

River, a distance of about 225 km. It was in Mossel Bay that the Europeans made their first contribution to South African history. After Bartholomeu Diaz had rounded the Cape of Good Hope, he dropped anchor offshore in order to replenish his water supply. He soon discovered a source of fresh water, but received a distinctly unfriendly reception from the native Hottentots who hurled stones at Diaz and his crew. Ten years later in 1488, the same tribe gave Vasco da Gama a much warmer welcome and the first business deal was struck. Da Gama exchanged some glass bead jewellery for an ox.

The city of Port Elizabeth in the Eastern Cape province, is the capital of the car industry. Despite the presence of numerous other industries and an advanced commercial infrastructure, which includes a modern harbour, the town is a very popular holiday destination. P.E., as it is often called, lies in Algoa Bay and boasts some magnificent beaches. The same is true of East London further up the coast. It was not founded, as you might imagine, by a bunch of Cockneys but by

German settlers. It is the only coastal town in South Africa with a river port.

The Atlantic coast is much drier than the lush, green landscape of the Indian Ocean coast, but it has its own stark, wild beauty. If you make the trip up to Langebaan lagoon and catch a glimpse of the old fishermen's huts at Churchhaven, you may be forgiven for thinking that you have stumbled across a Greek idyll. Here in the north-west is the Namaqualand region. Arid and barren for most of the year, in October, just after the rains, the coastal plain is transformed by millions of brightly coloured daisies, mesembryanthemums, aloes and lilies. The best view of this colourful array of wild flowers can be seen from Van Rhyn's Pass. Further north, straddling across the Botswana border, lies the Kalahari desert, with its wildlife park and famous Augrabies waterfalls.

CAPE TOWN

(A 6) Cape Town is considered by many to be one of the finest cities in the world. Its inhabitants are certainly convinced that it is. The harbour city shows its best side when approached by boat. The view from the sea encompasses the city set against the stunning backdrop of Table Mountain. In summer, a veil of cloud often descends on the huge flat-topped mountain and gradually dissipates as hot air rises. Equally fine is the view from Robben Island, formerly a prison, now a nature reserve. Trips out to the island include a visit to the cell where Nelson Mandela was incarcerated. On the city side of the bay lies the harbour. Given the dangerous inshore rocks, it was built well out to sea to provide vessels with enough depth for them to dock safely. The oldest part of the harbour, the Victoria and Alfred Waterfront, is now a restaurant and entertainment quarter.

Cape Town, often referred to as South Africa's Mother City, is the oldest town in the country. When Jan van Riebeeck arrived here with his fleet of three ships and 125 pioneers (only four of whom were women) the Dutch East India Company did not want to establish a proper settlement. All they wanted was a supply base for ships en route to the Far East. Some 27 years after Riebeeck's party disembarked, 700 people had settled here. With the appointment of Simon van der Stel as commander, immigrants were permitted to make their home at the Cape. Van der Stel remained in his post for 20 years, during which time he transformed the isolated trading centre into a flourishing colony.

Cape Town now boasts over 2 million inhabitants. After Johannesburg, it is the largest city in South Africa. Its main sources of income are tourism and the harbour, but it is also the republic's parliamentary capital. When the Union of South Africa was founded in 1910, it was decreed that Pretoria would be the seat of government, but that parliament would sit in Cape Town for six months of the year, from February onwards. So every year after Christmas, ministers, secretaries, civil servants, and foreign ambassadors, with their staff and families in tow, all migrate to the southern coast.

The inhabitants of Cape Town are a cheerful breed, renowned for their relaxed 'Mediterranean' disposition and their ability to enjoy life. Spoilt by the beauty of their natural surroundings, they refuse to allow the stresses and strains of urban life to take over and are never in a rush. Visitors from other less laid-back parts of the country call this state of mind 'Cape coma'. Business people from Johannesburg, for whom time is money, often become frustrated at the unhurried pace of life here. Anyone who has to drive the motorways of Johannesburg every day, will surely find the unique Capetonian patience, demonstrated on the narrow streets of the city, hard to contend with.

SIGHTS

Castle of Good Hope   **(I 5-6)**
This pentagonal fortification, built from Robben Island stone, was the residence of the Cape's first governor. Its original purpose was to protect the first settlers in the event of an attack. Begun in 1666 and completed in 1679, it is the oldest building

in South Africa. As well as housing the William Fehr Collection of Africana, it also serves as a military museum. Its most outstanding architectural feature is the baroque Kat Balcony which features plaster reliefs by Anton Anreith (c. 1790).

Daily 10.00-16.00 with guided tours every day at 10.00, 11.00, 12.00, 14.00 and 15.00; Castle St

Company's Garden (G 4)
Government Avenue, an oak-lined pedestrian street almost 6 km in length, starts near the Groote Kerk and links the inner city area with the suburbs at the foot of Table Mountain. On the right-hand side is a park known as Company's Garden. It was originally laid out in 1652 with fruit and vegetable gardens which supplied the passing trade ships.

Groot Constantia (O)
This historic vineyard estate is a fine example of Cape Dutch architecture. The mansion now houses a museum of 17th-century furniture, a collection of paintings and porcelain, and a wine museum. Constantia wines were served at European courts during Napoleon's time.

Restaurant and wine tasting Mon-Fri 09.00-16.30; museum daily 10.00-17.00; Groot Constantia Rd

Groote Kerk (H 4)
South Africa's oldest church stands at the end of Adderley Street. Originally completed in 1704, it was later rebuilt in 1841. The pulpit dating from 1788 is the work of the eminent sculptor, Anton Anreith.

Tues-Sat 10.30-12.00 and 14.00-15.00; Adderley St

Groot Constantia vineyard estate

Houses of Parliament and the Tuynhuis (G-H 4)
When parliament is in session during the summer and autumn, it is open to the public (on presentation of a passport). The Tuynhuis next door is now the president's official residence. Trees and plants from all over the world fill the grounds of the building which dates from 1571.

Guided tours July-Jan Mon-Fri 11.00-14.00; Government Ave

St George's Cathedral (H 4)
This cathedral was designed by the English architect, Sir Herbert Baker (1897-1901), who lived in South Africa for several years. It is the seat of the Anglican Archbishop of South Africa.

Wale St

Table Mountain and Kirstenbosch Botanical Garden (O)
★ ⚜ The breathtaking view from the top of the mountain (1086 m) encompasses all of the Cape peninsula. It only takes five minutes to reach the top by cable-car which operates every day, weather permitting (*Cable-car: Daily Dec-Apr 08.00-22.00, May-Nov 08.30-18.00; to see if the cable-car is running, check whether*

the green light on the cable-car mountain station is illuminated; Tel: 021/24 51 48).

The extensive ★ *Kirstenbosch Botanical Gardens* (560 hectares) are spread across the eastern slopes of Table Mountain at altitudes of between 100 and 1000 m. Almost all the 22 000 plant species native to South Africa are grown here. Attractions include a protea garden and scented garden. Tucked among the greenery is a small café which serves good food and refreshments. The best time to visit the gardens is in spring, ie August and September. (*Open daily from sunrise to sunset*)

Victoria and Alfred Waterfront (L 2)

The old wharf area has recently been transformed into one of Cape Town's biggest tourist attractions. Named after the British queen and her second son, Alfred, who laid the foundation stone for the new basin in 1860, the harbour is now surrounded by shops, restaurants, museums, a spectacular aquarium, hotels, theatres, bars, music venues and cinemas. An ideal way to round off a day of sightseeing is to sit at the quayside café with a glass of wine and watch the sun set. Alternatively, you could treat yourself to a sunset yacht cruise. *Tel: 021/418 23 69*

MUSEUMS

Koopmans de Wet House (I 4)

This historic house (1701) in Strand Street gives an insight into the lifestyle of the wealthy inhabitants of 18th-century Cape Town. It has one of the finest collections of Cape furniture.
Tues-Sat 09.30-16.30; 35 Strand St

Mayibye Centre for History and Culture in South Africa (O)

Pictures, posters and archive photographs of the apartheid era are displayed in this museum which is part of the University of the Western Cape in Bellville.
Modderdam Rd

South African Museum (G 4)

This natural history museum lies at the end of the Botanical Gardens. It has a varied collection, but the section which documents the life of the Bushmen is probably the most interesting.
Daily 10.00-17.00; Queen Victoria St

RESTAURANTS

Africa Café (O)

A good place to sample the different foods of the African continent.
213 Lower Main Rd; Category 3; Tel: 021/47 95 53

Blues (O)

◁▷ A fine view over the sea, beach and palm trees.
The Promenade, Victoria Rd/Camps Bay; Category 3; Tel: 021/438 20 40

Bonthuys (I 3)

The Belgian chef, Etienne Bonthuys, is the current favourite with Cape Town's gourmets. Always a surprise in store.
121 Castle St; Category 1; Tel: 021/26 23 68

Brass Bell (O)

Good restaurant renowned for its fish dishes. By the water's edge.
Kalk Bay Railway Station; Category 2; Tel: 021/788 54 55

Buitenverwachting (O)

One of the best restaurants in the city, if not the whole country.

Owned by the Buitenverwacht-ing estate.
Klein Constantia Rd; Category 1; Tel: 021/794 35 22

Floris Smit Huis (H 4)

Trendy meeting-place for the hip and chic.
55 Church St; Category 3; Tel: 021/23 34 14

La Perla (0)

Popular fish restaurant by the sea with a predominantly Italian menu. Open all day.
Corner of Beach Rd and Church Rd; Category 2; Tel: 021/434 24 71

SHOPPING

Cape Town's Golden Acre is the biggest underground shopping mall in the southern hemisphere, where you can buy anything and everything.

Native arts and crafts made by the many ethnic tribes are sold at the daily flea market (*08.00-16.00, except Sun*) on the lovely Green Market Square, an atmospheric market place that dates back to the 17th-century. St George's Street pedestrianized zone and the adjoining passages are lined with the city's smartest shops. For antiques and bric-à-brac explore Long Street and Church Street.

Green Point flea market (0)

Every Sunday, traders from all parts of the country set up their stalls in the car park in front of the stadium.

HOTELS

The Bay (0)

A modern hotel beside one of the finest beaches in Camps Bay. No room is smaller than 40 sq m. The penthouse rooms are among the most luxurious in South Africa.
70 rooms; Beach Rd; Category 2; Tel: 021/438 44 44, Fax: 438 44 55

The Breakwater Lodge (L 1)

An inexpensive and central spot by the water's edge.
300 rooms; Portswood Rd; Category 3; Tel: 021/406 19 11, Fax: 406 10 70

The Cellars-Hohenort (0)

Exclusive hotel in the Constantia wine-making region. Close to the Kirstenbosch Botanical Gardens.
43 rooms; 15 Hohenort Ave; Category 1; Tel: 021/794 21 37, Fax: 794 21 49

Mount Nelson (0)

Built in 1899, this luxury-class colonial hotel stands in the middle of a large garden close to the city centre. Winston Churchill drank tea on the terrace here while

---

In the Marco Polo Spirit

Marco Polo was the first true world traveller. He travelled with peaceful intentions forging links between the East and the West. His aim was to discover the world, and explore different cultures and environments without changing or disrupting them. He is an excellent role model for the 20th-century traveller. Wherever we travel we should show respect for other peoples and the natural world.

WWF

working as a newspaper reporter during the Boer War.

159 rooms; Orange St; Category 1; Tel: 021/23 10 00, Fax: 24 74 72

SPORT & LEISURE

Sailing boats and yachts can be hired in the harbour (*reservations: 021/418 23 69*), or you can go deep-sea fishing (*Tel: 021/64 22 03*). Many beaches are ideal for surfing or windsurfing (*Tel: 021/419 18 14*). Golfing enthusiasts should enquire at the *Royal Cape Golf Club* (*Tel: 021/761 65 51*).

Clifton   (O)
✸ Of the main beaches in Cape Town, the four Clifton beaches are the finest. They are all sheltered from the wind and ideal for sunbathing and windsurfing. Swimming is for the more courageous – the temperature of the water in the Atlantic Ocean never rises above 17°C.

ENTERTAINMENT

⚐ ✸ The waterfront, harbour and Sea Point areas are always busy at night. There are so many restaurants around here you could eat in a different one every day of the year. There are also plenty of night-clubs in the area, though none are particularly recommendable. At night, the 300-m high ⌁ Signal Hill affords a fine view over Cape Town.

INFORMATION

Captour   (I 4)
Adderley St; Tel: 021/418 52 14, Fax: 418 52 27

SURROUNDING AREA

Bloubergstrand   (A 6)
A famous battle between the British and the Boers, which culminated in the second occupation of the Cape by Crown forces, took place here in 1806. The town offers a fine view of Table Mountain and Cape Town.

Bloubergstrand or 'blue mountain beach' acquired its name because, when viewed from here, Table Mountain often looks as if it is shrouded in a blue haze. The beach offers ideal conditions for windsurfing and angling. A former fisherman's hut has been

The view of Table Mountain from Bloubergstrand is stunning

converted into the popular *Restaurant Ons Huisie*. It has a good reputation for fish (*Stadler Rd; Category 2; Tel: 021/56 15 53*).

Cape of Good Hope (A 6)

★ ◁▷ The Cape of Good Hope lies at the southern tip of the Cape peninsula. Contrary to popular belief, however, it is not Africa's most southerly point. If you want to see the place where the Indian and Atlantic Oceans officially meet, you will have to go 200 km further east to Cape Agulhas. The Cape of Good Hope promontory has been designated a nature reserve and its majestic landscape is home to many wild animals including rare antelope, Cape mountain zebra, *bontebok* and *eland* that graze on the sandy plateau. After he rounded the treacherous peninsula for the first time, Bartholomeu Diaz named it the Cape of Storms because of the strong winds that whip around it. Before setting out for this spectacular landmark, it's always a good idea to check the weather forecast. A cable-car runs from the car-park at the end of the road up to *Cape Point* (40 m). You will have to climb the last few metres (133 steps), but your efforts will be rewarded by a breathtaking view over the sea, *False Bay* and the Cape peninsula. The old lighthouse, which dates from 1836, was abandoned a long time ago. A little lower down, stands the new lighthouse (1919) which guides some 20 000 vessels around the Cape every year. In fine weather the Cape beaches are perfect for picnics. Alternatively, you can stop off on your way back at the *Camel Rock Restaurant* in the village of Scarborough.

Chapman's Peak Drive (A 6)

◁▷ Carved out of the rock in the 1920s this winding road which runs from Hout Bay to the Cape of Good Hope, ranks among the finest coast roads in the world. With the rocks towering above and the sea raging below, the scenery on the 10 km drive is stunning. Horses are available for hire in Nordhoek, a small town beneath the summit of Chapman's Peak.

Simonstown (A 6)

This town was once the biggest base for the British navy in the southern hemisphere. It is still reminiscent of an English port, even though it is now the headquarters of the South African marines. The main street reveals the town's historic past; 21 of the houses are over 150 years old.

CALEDON

(**B 6**) At around the turn of the century, the springs in Caledon, six warm and one cold, drew visitors from all over Europe. The spectacular Victorian hotel that once stood in the town was destroyed by fire in 1946. It was 1990 before a replacement was built on the same spot. Caledon is a popular base for walkers.

SIGHTS

Victoria Wild Flower and Garden Reserve

If you are interested in flowers and gardens, then set aside at least half a day for this botanical extravaganza. An unbelievable range of flowers is crammed into 10 hectares.
Mon-Sat 08.30-17.00

Caledon Museum

Focuses on life in South Africa during the reign of Queen Victoria. One of the nine cannons which the early farmers used to defend their territory stands outside the museum.

Mon-Fri 08.00-17.00, Sat 09.00-12.00; 11 Krige St

Overberger

↘ A country hotel where you can relax in warm spring water in a Victorian bath.

95 rooms; Nerina Ave; Category 3; Tel: 0281/412 70, Fax: 412 71

Caledon Municipality

22 Plein St; Tel: 0281/215 11

Arniston (Waenhuiskrans) (B 6)

An old fishing town surrounded by impressive sand dunes. Some vast caves, about a kilometre away, can be explored at low tide.

Arniston Hotel (situated by the beach); 55 rooms; Category 2; Tel: 028 47/590 00, Fax: 596 33

Cape Agulhas (B 6)

Although not quite so spectacular as the Cape of Good Hope, this peninsula is the southern-most point of Africa. The Portuguese word *agulhas* means 'needles' and is thought to be a reference to the abundance of small jagged rocks and reefs that are so hazardous for ships. The lighthouse, which dates from 1848, is open to visitors *daily from 11.00 to 15.00.*

Cape Agulhas – the southernmost tip of the continent

The intensity of its beam is equivalent to the light of 11 million candles.

Hermanus (B 6)

Set in a delightful spot on the Atlantic coast, lined with lovely beaches, Hermanus is one of South Africa's most popular and fashionable holiday resorts. For Capetonians, it is the ideal place for a weekend on the beach and, during the summer months, it is a hive of activity. The ✪ *De Mond* lagoon at the mouth of the small river is a haven for watersports enthusiasts. Anglers regard the offshore waters here as among the best in South Africa. Between July and November whales migrate to Walker Bay to mate and give birth. *The Marine* is a delightful harbourside hotel (*32 rooms; Category 3; Tel: 0283/70 10 00, Fax: 70 01 60*) and *The Burgundy* (*Market Square; Category 2; Tel: 0283/228 00*) is unquestionably the best restaurant in town.

Sir Lowry's Pass (B 6)

↘ The panorama from this mountain pass is outstanding.

Once a staging post and livery stable, the historic *Howhoek Inn* is said to be the oldest hotel in South Africa. It is surrounded by magnificent gardens (*18 rooms; Category 3; Tel: 02824/496 46, Fax: 491 12*).

EAST LONDON

(**E 5**) Even the inhabitants of East London (pop. 200 000) take their holidays here. With such magnificent beaches and an average of seven hours of sunshine per day, why go anywhere else? At the beginning of the colonial era, the town marked the border between the British settlers and the Xhosa tribes. The territorial wars that raged between 1779 and 1838 claimed the lives of many warriors and the tribal leaders were in a state of desperation. In 1856, a nine-year-old girl called Nongquase prophesied that if the Xhosas sacrificed all their crops and animals, then their ancestors would come and drive all the white invaders into the sea. She was taken at her word and, as a result, some 20 000 tribesmen and women died of hunger and the 40 000 survivors were forced off their land. Nongquase was later arrested, imprisoned on Robben Island and then exiled to the Eastern Cape where she died in 1898. Until the arrival of 2400 German settlers in 1857, East London was principally a military base. The Germans, who had aided the British during the sixth frontier war and who originally intended to fight for Queen Victoria in the Crimean War, decided to disband and settle here, adding to the already cosmopolitan mix of the region. Place-names such as

Berlin, Hamburg, Potsdam, Stutterheim and Braunschweig bear witness to the German roots of many of today's inhabitants.

SIGHTS

German Settlers' Memorial
The first Europeans to settle in this important port came from Germany and this monument recalls their contribution to its development. The bronze sculpture by Lipschitz depicts a family leaving their German homeland. *Esplanade*

Harbour
The John Baillie Memorial commemorates the man who first hoisted the British flag here. *Guided tours through the harbour are organized by the Greater East London Publicity Association; City Hall, Oxford St; Tel: 0431/260 15*

MUSEUM

East London Museum
This natural history museum has a very rare exhibit. Found at the mouth of the Chalumna River in 1938, the coelacanth is a primitive fish thought to have been extinct for 60 million years. What makes it so fascinating are its fins which resemble stumpy legs. As well as the preserved coelacanth, the museum also keeps the only known example of a dodo's egg. This large flightless bird has been extinct for many years. An anthropological section in the museum documents the tribal traditions of the Xhosas from the neighbouring Transkei and Ciskei regions. *Mon-Fri 09.30-17.00, Sat 09.30-12.00; 319 Oxford St*

RESTAURANT

The Prawn Inn
There are some very good fish restaurants in the harbour area. The Prawn Inn is one of the best-known.
Cliffort St; Category 2; Tel: 0431/ 242 53

SHOPPING

Lock Street Gaol
The last execution took place here in 1935. The death cells and gallows are open to the public, but the rest of the cells in the old town jail, built in 1880, are now occupied by traders selling handicrafts and souvenirs.
Lock St

HOTEL

Kennaway
A good hotel right by the sea.
88 rooms; Beach Front; Category 2; Tel: 0431/255 31, Fax: 213 26

SPORT & LEISURE

Diving
The seabed is scattered with shipwrecks. On 26 May 1872 alone, seven vessels sank off East London and the local diving fraternity are on an endless search for valuable cargo.

For further information, Tel: 0431/ 249 21

Windsurfing, sailing
The artificial lake of the Bridal Drift Dam provides excellent opportunities for windsurfing, sailing and canoeing. Overnight accommodation is available in cabins. The nature reserve is a haven for bird-watchers.
Tel: 0431/254 24

INFORMATION

The East London Publicity Association
Old Library Building, Argyle St; Tel: 0431/260 15

SURROUNDING AREA

King William's Town   (D 5)
Originally a missionary station, King William's Town (or 'King' as it is called by its inhabitants) was destroyed by Xhosa warriors in 1835. Once the British had established a military base here, the missionaries returned and founded the town. In 1858, 2000 German settlers arrived in the hope of making a new life for themselves, but many of them died of starvation. The *Kaffrarian Museum* has a section devoted to the early German settlers, and it also focuses on the influence of

---

Show Houses
One popular Sunday afternoon activity for South Africans is visiting 'show houses'. Home-owners wishing to sell their property allow estate agents to show prospective buyers around their property on Sunday afternoons. Even people who have no intention of buying, however, will pop in to have a good look round out of pure curiosity – there is something fascinating about seeing other people's houses and catching a glimpse of the way they live.

the Xhosa and the British on the region's development. The *South African Missionary Museum* documents the work and influence of missionaries in southern Africa.

Wild Coast   (E 5)

The Wild Coast is a beautiful 250 km stretch of rugged coast which boasts some magnificent, often deserted beaches. Its name is actually rather misleading, as these beaches are perfectly safe and rank among the finest in South Africa. Scattered between the rolling green hills, beside lagoons and rivers, are the round, white huts of the Xhosa tribes. One of the larger towns in this region is Port St Johns at the mouth of the Umzimvubu River. If you wander along the rocks and cliffs, you will probably pass groups of local women selling fish and oysters. *Wild Coast Sun Hotel* is one of the best hotels in the chain. Not only does it offer first-class gastronomy, but its facilities also include a casino and a golf course overlooking the sea.
Between the mouth of the Umtavuna and Mzamba rivers; Category 1; Tel: 0471/591 11, Fax: 529 24

The Huguenot Museum in Franschhoek

FRANSCHHOEK

(B 6) The principal activity of this little town, situated in a beautiful valley, is centred around the production of wine. It was founded in 1688 by 146 Huguenots, who had fled from France following the prohibition of Protestantism by the Catholic majority. They called their new home *Le Quartier Français* – the French quarter. Many of the new settlers originated from the wine-growing regions of France. Given the similar climate, they soon began to cultivate vineyards, which have subsequently become very successful. The wine-growers in and around the Franschhoek area have formed a collective known as the Vignerons de Franschhoek. Almost all the vineyard estates offer wine tasting.
For further information, call 021/876 20 86

SIGHTS

Franschhoek Pass

Probably the finest mountain pass in the region, it affords a splendid view over the valley. The first settlers called it Elephants' Pass, because the track was used by elephants and other herds of animals crossing the mountains.

Haute Provence

This estate is renowned for producing good wines at reasonable prices. The owner, Peter Younghusband, also an international journalist, keeps his collection of paintings by renowned South African artists in the room where wine tasting sessions are held.
Tel: 021/876 31 95

MUSEUM

Huguenot Memorial Museum

Tells the fascinating story of the Huguenots and the first settlers.
Mon-Sat 08.00-17.00, Sun 14.00-17.00; Lambrecht St

RESTAURANTS

Haute Cabrière

〰️ Marvellous restaurant above a wine cellar carved out of the hillside. Seated against a rocky backdrop, you can admire the splendid view of the Franschhoek valley while enjoying a delicious meal and a bottle of the celebrated Cabrière wine.
Pass Rd; Category 2; Tel: 021/876 36 88

La Petite Ferme

〰️ Country restaurant on the Franschhoek Pass. Enjoy the view over lunch or a snack.
Pass Rd; Category 3; Tel: 021/876 30 16

HOTEL

Le Quartier Français

Small country hotel that backs on-to a restaurant of the same name.
17 rooms; Berg St; Category 2; Tel: 021/876 21 51, Fax: 876 31 05

INFORMATION

Franschhoek Tourist Information

La Maison Antique, Huguenot Rd; Tel: 021/876 36 30

SURROUNDING AREA

Boschendal (B 6)

Set in the beautiful Drakenstein valley, this vineyard is one of South Africa's finest. The estate was founded by the Huguenot de Villiers family, who lived here for over 200 years until the end of the last century. It now belongs to the Anglo-American minerals company. The estate mansion has been turned into a *museum*, which is furnished in the traditional Cape residential style (*Daily 11.00-16.00*). In the *restaurant* next door you can sample the widely acclaimed Boschendal wine (*Tel: 021/874 12 52*). This is a lovely spot for a summer picnic in the shade of the tall trees.
Wine sampling Mon-Fri 08.30-17.00, Sat 08.30-12.30; Category 3

Paarl (B 6)

Paarl is the largest town in the Cape Town hinterland. Founded in 1717, it was named after a nearby rock that looks like a giant pearl when the sun shines on it from a certain direction. KWV, the biggest wine co-operative in South Africa, is based here and the wine and brandy cellars in *Kohler Street* are said to be the largest in the world (*Guided tours and wine tasting Mon, Wed and Fri 11.00 and 15.45, Tues and Thurs 09.00 and 14.15*). Directly opposite, the *Laborie Restaurant*, serves local wines and traditional fare (*Category 3; Tel: 021/807 30 95*).

Paarl played a central role in the development of Afrikaans and *Paarl Publicity Association* (*216 Main Rd; Tel: 021/802 38 29*) organizes guided tours through the historic town. The *Hotel Grande Roche*, one of the oldest wine estates in Paarl, combines traditional five-star comfort with excellent cuisine. A stay here is an unforgettable experience (*35 suites; 225 Main St; Category 1; Tel: 021/863 27 27, Fax: 863 22 20*).

Tulbagh (B 6)

This historic town in the heart of the fruit-growing region is noted for its many Cape Dutch houses. Every building in Church Street is under a preservation order. An earthquake struck Tulbagh in 1969 and the town was almost completely destroyed but, lovingly and at great expense, it has slowly been rebuilt. The *Oude Kerk* or the Old Church houses a collection of church pews, dating from different centuries. Some still bear the names of the local dignitaries, for whom they were reserved. ⚮ The *Paddagang* restaurant in Tulbagh is a wonderful place to relax in. You can sit in its garden under spreading trees and vines, surrounded by roses, and enjoy traditional Cape dishes.
Church St; Category 3; Tel: 0236/30 02 42

GEORGE

(C 6) The capital of the Garden Route is situated at the foot of the Outeniqua Mountains. Not far from the sea, it is surrounded by a green and fertile cultivated landscape. Visitors arriving here from the interior will have crossed the mountains via the Montagu or Outeniqua Pass, which was built by Italian prisoners-of-war during World War II. The town itself is very pretty. As you stroll around, keep an eye out for the old library in York Street. One of the oak trees in front of the building has been placed under a conservation order – known as the *Old Slave Tree*, it marks the spot where slaves were sold. Also on York Street is *St Mark's Cathedral*, said to be the smallest cathedral on the continent.

SIGHTS

Outeniqua Choo Tjoe

The journey from George to Knysna on this steam train is a memorable three-hour excursion. The line passes through tunnels, across lagoons, rivers and lakes and alongside the sea.
Mon-Fri, Sat services during the holidays; tickets sold at the station

MUSEUM

George Museum

Formerly the courthouse, this museum focuses on the local timber industry, explaining the history of its development and processing methods. Much of the furniture is made from African hardwood, such as *yellowwood* and *stinkwood*. There is also a collection of musical instruments.
Mon-Fri 09.00-16.30, Sat 09.00-12.30; Old Drostdy Building, Courtenay St

RESTAURANTS

Copper Pot

🌸 Very popular with the locals.
Multi Center, Mead St; Category 2; Tel: 0441/74 31 91

Old Town House

Excellent fish dishes. The sole is particularly good.
Market St; Category 2; Tel: 0441/74 36 63

HOTEL

Fancourt

This splendid country mansion built in the 1860s is surrounded by a golf course designed by the South African golfing hero, Gary Player. The extensive 27-hole

course is open to guests.
86 rooms; Montagu St; Category 2; Tel: 0441/70 82 82, Fax: 70 76 05

George is a popular destination for walkers. The 8-day Outeniqua Hiking Trail starts here. Tourists are also drawn here for the magnificent Indian Ocean beaches, while Victoria Bay is a prime spot for surfers.

INFORMATION

George Information Service
Civic Centre; Tel: 0441/74 40 00

SURROUNDING AREA

Cango Caves   (C 6)
★ These vast underground caverns are among the finest stalactite and stalagmite caves in the world. Reckoned to be at least 25 million years old, they present a unique and quite stunning interplay between shape and colour.
A guided tour lasts two hours; daily at 09.00, 11.00, 13.00 and 15.00

Mossel Bay   (C 6)
Mossel Bay is named after the abundance of shellfish European sailors found in its waters when they first came here 400 years ago. After 20 years of exploration, oil was finally discovered here and what was once a picturesque port and holiday resort, has been spoilt to a large extent by the rigs and processing plants. Mossel Bay is famous for being South Africa's first post office. It all started in the 16th century when a sailor put a written report of his voyage in a boot which he then hung in a milkwood tree. His 'letter' was subsequently found and read by other mariners who came after him. From then on sailors would leave letters here to be picked up by ships that were homeward bound. Any letter posted in the boot-shaped post box which stands here today is given a special postmark. Near the post box is the freshwater spring which it is said, Diaz used to replenish his ship's water tanks. Those with an interest in maritime history should visit the *Bartholomeu Diaz Museum (Mon-Fri 09.00-12.30 and 14.00-15.45)*. If you need a hotel try the *Eight Bells on the Mountain Inn* on the main road between Mossel Bay and Oudtshoorn (*24 rooms; Category 2; Tel: 0444/95 15 44, Fax: 95 15 48*).

Oudtshoorn   (C 6)
Oudtshoorn is the world centre for ostrich rearing. These huge flightless birds are bred more successfully here than anywhere else. Even before World War I, local farmers were making a fortune from the sale of ostrich feathers, which were fashion accessories for the wealthy. Demand is still high. Every nine months the ostrich loses its feathers, shedding about a kilo of plumage. Ostriches are also farmed for meat and leather which is made into shoes, belts, wallets, purses etc. It is claimed that the oldest ostrich in Oudtshoorn reached the age of 81. There are two *farms* where visitors are welcome: *Highgate Tel: 0443/22 71 15* and *Safari Tel: 0443/22 73 11; both open daily 07.30-17.00*. While in the area, why not try an ostrich steak or an omelette made with ostrich eggs. The *C.P. Nel Museum* documents the history of ostrich breeding

Oudtshoorn is the world's main ostrich-farming centre

(*Mon-Sat 14.00-17.00, Sun 14.30-17.00; Baron von Rheede St*).

GRAAFF-REINET

(**C 5**) Graaff-Reinet is one of two towns in the world which lie within the boundaries of a nature reserve. Surrounded by the *Karoo Nature Reserve*, the town is often described as the jewel of the Karoo. Founded in 1786 by Boer settlers, Graaff-Reinet is actually one of the oldest settlements in South Africa. It was named after the governor Cornelis Jacob van der Graaff and his wife, Cornelia Reinet. The town centre is like a large open-air museum, displaying all the architectural styles prevalent over the last 200 years. The buildings range from the simple, flat single-storey Karoo hut to the gabled Cape Dutch residences and late Victorian houses. All have been lavishly restored. There are around 300 or more historic buildings in Graaff-Reinet, and all of them pre-date any building in Johannesburg.

MUSEUM

Reinet House and Museum
Beautiful Cape Dutch-style house with 18th- and 19th-century furniture, and huge vine in courtyard. *Mon-Fri 09.00-12.00 and 15.00-17.00, Sat/Sun 10.00-12.00; Murray St*

HOTEL

Drostdy Hotel
This splendid hotel occupies one of the oldest and finest buildings in Graaff-Reinet. Originally the National Assembly, it was built in 1806 by the eminent architect, Thibauld, whose work you will come across throughout the Cape provinces. After decades of decay and neglect, work started on its restoration in the 1970s. It has now been restored to its former glory. It is worth treating yourself to a night here and a romantic candelit dinner which is served in the old courtroom.
51 rooms; 28 Church St; Category 3; Tel: 0491/221 61, Fax: 245 82

Huberta

The prized exhibit in the Kaffrarian Museum in King William's Town is a stuffed hippopotamus. Nothing particularly special about that you may think, but between 1928 and 1931, Hubert, as he was christened, captured the imagination of the whole country. He first appeared in Zululand. From there he set out on a journey of several hundred kilometres with several changes in direction. He emerged in the most unusual of places at the most unusual of times. One morning, the creature was seen in the centre of Durban. Sadly Hubert met a violent death when he was accidentally shot by a farmer. Only when Hubert was dead did his followers discover that the wandering hippo was in fact a 'she'. Hubert was renamed Huberta.

ENTERTAINMENT

♣ In the evenings farmers from the surrounding area congregate in both hotel bars. Wednesday is a popular night with the locals – you might even catch some can-can dancing.

INFORMATION

Graaff-Reinet Publicity Association
Church St; Tel: 0491/224 79

SURROUNDING AREA

Karoo National Park (B-C 4)
Springboks, wildebeest and other wildlife thrive in this 33 000-hectare reserve. ◁▷ The *Valley of Desolation* is an unusual geological phenomenon. Formed over 200 million years by erosion, it is more of a gorge than a valley with its steep strangely-shaped rocks that rise sharply to a height of 120 m. (Anyone found removing fossils will be punished with a hefty fine). There are various viewpoints in the area that offer stunning panoramas of the surrounding country. A number of walking trails run through the reserve.

KIMBERLEY

(D 4) The discovery in 1866 of the first sparkling rock on the banks of the Orange River triggered the biggest diamond rush of all time, transforming a simple farming community into the capital of South Africa's diamond industry. This piece of rock picked up by a young boy, yielded a 22-carat diamond which was named 'Eureka'. It can still be seen in the town's mining museum. In the early days, it was only the locals who went in search of the precious stones but it wasn't long before the place was flooded with fortune-seekers who came here from all over the world. Diamonds were discovered beside the river and deep in the ground. A shanty town quickly sprang up to house the many thousands of diamond hunters and the new settlement was named New Rush. In 1870, some 30 000 people set about digging what is now the largest man-made crater in the world. The *Big Hole* has a circumference of 4572 m, a diameter of 1.5 km and is 800 m deep. Initially it was every man for himself, but eventually some semblance of order was brought to the diggings and individual miners were forced to form syndicates. Gradually these developed into large companies.

Over a period of 43 years, three tonnes of diamonds were extracted from the rocks. The shanty town huts were gradually replaced by more substantial dwellings and in 1873 the settlement was renamed Kimberley. The giant Johannesburg-based multinational De Beers Consolidated Mines company had its beginnings in Kimberley when diamonds were discovered on the *De Beers farm*. Some engaging figures made their fortune here. Cecil Rhodes, originally an English parson's son, acquired many claims, including those belonging to the de Beers family, and the former English boxer and actor, Barney Barnato, also made a huge fortune. Kimberley prospered too, becoming the first town to have such luxuries as electric street lighting and trams. The first stock exchange and a flying school were founded here. South Africa's prosperity owes a lot not just to the fortuitous discovery of mineral wealth, but also to the entrepreneurs and pioneers.

SIGHTS

Big Hole and Kimberley Museum
A reconstructed mining village consisting of the original tin shanty town that existed at the time of the great rush has been built beside the worked-out Big Hole. A number of viewing points offer visitors an opportunity of surveying the vast crater. The museum's collection of diamonds is one of the finest in the

world. One, known simply as the 616 because of its 616 carats, is thought to be the largest uncut diamond ever found.
Daily 08.00-18.00; Bultfontein St

Bultfontein Diamond Recovery Plant
A modern diamond mine.
Guided tours daily 09.00 and 11.00; Molyneux Rd; Tel: 0531/296 51

Steam Locomotive Shunting Yards
Some 40 old steam locomotives used at the Kimberley mines can be seen in the former sidings and at Witput station.
Oliver St; Tel: 0531/288 20 61

Tram Service
Trams carry visitors from the City Hall to the Big Hole along the original track which dates from 1913. Buy your ticket on board the tram.
Daily 09.00-16.00

MUSEUM

McGregor Museum
Built by Cecil Rhodes as a sanatorium, the building gives some indication of how the hugely wealthy diamond barons once lived. It also documents the history and environment of the Northern Cape.
Mon-Fri 09.00-17.00, Sat 09.00-13.00, Sun 14.00-17.00; Egerton Rd

RESTAURANTS

Halfway House Hotel Drive-In Pub
When this pub first opened in 1880, clients arrived on horseback. Now they can pick up their drink without getting out of the car.
229 Du Toitspan Rd; Category 3; Tel: 0531/251 51

Star of the West Pub

This bar is one of the oldest in South Africa. One of the bar stools was made specially for Cecil Rhodes.
On the tram route; Category 3; Tel: 0531/264 63

HOTELS

Edgerton House

Directly opposite the McGregor Museum, this hotel is now a listed building.
13 rooms; 5 Egerton Rd; Category 3; Tel: 0531/81 18 71, Fax: 81 17 85

Savoy Hotel

A grand hotel which combines old-world charm with modern comforts.
42 rooms; De Beers Rd; Category 2; Tel: 0531/262 11

INFORMATION

Kimberley Publicity Office

City Hall, Old Main St; Tel: 0531/272 98

SURROUNDING AREA

Augrabies Falls (B 4)

The name Augrabies derives from the Hottentot language and means 'place of the great noise', a reference to the first stage of the falls where the Orange River drops 56 m into a 20-m wide gorge. The waters crash into a deep lake (130 m) sending a vast column of spray into the air, enveloping the whole area in mist. Rumour has it that a horde of diamonds washed away by the river lies on the bed of the lake, but the sheer volume and depth of water has deterred divers from trying to find out the truth. In times of drought, the flow is not so great, but occasional flash floods cause the river to burst its banks and the falls turn into a frightening torrent. The sight of this sheer ravine and thundering cascade in the stark desert landscape is quite spectacular.

Barkly West (C 4)

The hunt for diamonds began in Barkly West after the discovery of diamonds here in 1869. Prospectors still come in the hope of stumbling across some priceless gem. If you want to seek your fortune here, you must first obtain a licence from the local police station (June to September only). On Saturdays, diamond dealers still come to town to see if the treasure-seekers have unearthed anything worth buying. An open-air archaeological museum displays ancient artefacts uncovered by diamond miners during excavations.
Daily 09.00-16.00

Kalahari Gemsbok National Park (B 3)

★ This national park is the largest unspoilt ecosystem in the world. When combined with the Botswana National Park, it covers an area of over 2 million hectares. It is a semi-arid and seemingly inhospitable habitat, but it teems with wildlife. Lions, cheetahs and jackals hunt among the herds of gemsbok, springbok and impala. The park is open throughout the year, but the best time to visit is between March and May or September and October. Overnight accommodation is available in three camps.
On the B3 past Upington towards Botswana; Tel: 012/343 19 91

Plettenberg Bay – where luxury holiday homes overlook the beach

KNYSNA

(C 6) This attractive and colourful town occupying a marvellous spot between wooded mountains, a large lagoon and the sea, is one of the most popular destinations on the Garden Route. It was founded in 1804 by George Rex. His lavish lifestyle fuelled rumours that he was the illegitimate son of George III and that he had been forced to leave Britain after his father surprisingly became king. One of George Rex's ships was the first vessel to cut through into the lagoon from the sea. The opening is flanked by two great sandstone rocks known as the *Knysna Heads*. The oysters farmed in this 13 sq km lagoon are believed to be among the best in the world.

Knysna Forest

This forest, the biggest area of woodland in South Africa, extends for over 170 km from George eastwards along the Outeniqua and Tsitsikamma Mountains. It has many giant yellowwood trees and stinkwood trees, some of which are as old as 800 years. In places the forest is so dense it could almost be described as jungle. It is a habitat for numerous different bird species and the few remaining Knysna elephants.

MUSEUM

Millwood House Museum

An exhibition documenting the history of the town and its founder, George Rex.
Quenens St; Mon-Fri 10.00-12.00

SIGHTS

King Edward Tree

This giant yellowwood tree in Knysna Forest is 600 years old. It has a 6 m circumference and rises to an incredible height of 40 m.

RESTAURANTS

Jetty Tapas

⊛ Situated by the pier, this is the perfect place for oysters.
Thesen's Jetty; Category 3; Tel: 0445/ 219 27

La Loerie

Named after the famous bird found in this area.
Main Rd; Category 2; Tel: 0445/216 16

Pink Umbrella

Garden restaurant only open in the summer for lunch and tea.
King's Way Leisure; Category 3; Tel: 0445/227 31

HOTELS

Belvidere Manor

𝒗 Excellent hotel set in a historic country house with a view over the lagoon and the woods.
30 cottages; Belvidere Estate; Category 2; Tel: 0445/387 10 55, Fax: 387 10 59

Portland Manor

Country manor above Knysna, set in the middle of a park with its own lake.
10 rooms; Via Rheenendal Rd; Category 3; Tel 0445/48 04, Fax: 48 63

SPORT & LEISURE

Elephant Walk

This 21 km-long waymarked trail through the Knysna Forest begins in Knysna. It is a long, but pleasant walk which passes the King Edward Tree (see page 53). If a day-long hike sounds too much like hard work, there are two shorter alternatives.

House-boats

The lagoon offers all kinds of watersports facilities. For an unforgettable experience, stay overnight in one of the house-boats, which are available for rent.
Lightley's in Bluewaters; Category 3; Tel: 0445/87 10 26

INFORMATION

Knysna Publicity Association

40 Main St; Tel: 0445/216 10

SURROUNDING AREA

Plettenberg Bay (C 4)

★ When the Portuguese explorer, Mesquita da Perestrelo, came ashore here in 1576, he was struck by the beauty of the place and called it the Bahia Formosa, 'beautiful bay'. It was rechristened in 1778 by the Dutch governor Joachim van Plettenberg, who was equally charmed and gave it his own name. Plettenberg Bay has developed into an exclusive resort. It boasts three magnificent beaches which extend for 11 km. The warm, shallow water is ideal for children and the sun shines on average 320 days in the year. Between July and September, whales come into the bay to give birth to their young. The former whaling station has been converted into a 3-star hotel: 𝒗 *Beacon Island* stands on a peninsula overlooking the sea where whales and dolphins swim and dive (*200 rooms; Category 2; Tel: 04457/311 20, Fax: 338 80*). The 𝒗 *Plettenberg* above the beach also enjoys a sweeping view of the Indian Ocean. It is elegant, but smaller and more intimate than Beacon Island (*40 rooms; Category 1; Tel: 04457/320 30, Fax: 320 74*).

There are two restaurants worth recommending in 'Plett': one is the *Islander*, reputedly the best fish restaurant in South Africa (*Category 2; Tel: 04457/77 76*); the other is ☻ *The 7 Cellars*, where just reading the wine list will stimulate the taste buds (*Category 3; Tel: 04457/ 320 60*).

Tsitsikamma
Coastal National Park (C 6)

This nature reserve extends for over 100 km from Plettenberg as far as the mouth of the Groot River. The protected zone includes not only the coastal belt but also a 5-km wide strip of the inshore waters. Further inland in the Tsitsikamma Forest National Park, a section of huge primeval forest has survived. Particularly impressive is the ⚐ *Paul Sauer Bridge* which spans the Storms River 130m above. If you want to spend a night in this green and beautiful environment, then make enquiries at the *Tsitsikamma Forest Inn. 20 cottages; Stormsriver; Category 3; Tel 042/541 17 11, Fax: 541 16 69.*

LANGEBAAN

(**A 5**) About 16 km long, 5 km wide, and only 6 m deep, the warm waters of the Langebaan lagoon draw flocks of aquatic birds, around 55 000 in the summer months, including flamingos and cormorants. The small town at the end of the lagoon attracts watersports enthusiasts, especially anglers and divers.

SIGHTS

Churchhaven
Romantic fishing village with old houses by the lagoon.

HOTEL

Farmhouse Langebaan
Part of the hotel is in an old farmhouse which enjoys a fine view over the lagoon. You can watch the dolphins and flamingos from the terrace.

28 rooms; 5 Egret St; Category 3; Tel: 02287/220 62, Fax: 219 80

SURROUNDING AREA

Saldanha (A 5)
This town was named after a Portuguese general, who landed here in 1503 and quickly appreciated its strategic importance. If Saldanha had found water here, the town would probably have developed into a more important port than Cape Town, as the bay makes an excellent natural harbour and is well placed for the export of iron ore. The restaurants in the harbour area serve simple, but delicious fish dishes. *Guided tours of the harbour every Wed at 10.00 (meet at the loading terminal); Tel: 02281/355 72 95*

MATJIESFONTEIN

(**B 5**) This Victorian village stands on the edge of the semi-arid Karoo – a Hottentot word meaning 'drought'. Traditional windwheels mark the spots where bore holes yield water. Vegetation is so sparse that only sheep rearing is feasible and the sheep farms cover huge tracts of land.

Matjiesfontein was originally a small station for farmers from the surrounding countryside. In 1876 the young Scot, James Douglas Logan settled here. The respiratory illness he had been suffering from since childhood was cured by the dry climate. He therefore set about turning Matjiesfontein into a spa and holiday resort. His attempts were successful and many people came here including such illustrious figures as Lord Randolph Churchill and the Sultan of Zanzibar. The town has

A journey on the luxury Blue Train is an unforgettable experience

changed little since Logan's time. As it passes through Matjiesfontein, the Blue Train nearly always blows its whistle and the locals drinking in the town's only bar can be relied upon to toot back in unison.

MUSEUM

Mary Rawdon Museum
This small museum, with a collection of Victoriana, brings to life the horrors of the Boer War.
Mon-Sat 09.00-9.30 and 17.00-17.30, Sun 09.30-10.30 and 17.00-17.30; Logan St

HOTELS

Lord Milner
Elegant rooms in a traditional Victorian hotel. Formal dining.
28 rooms; Logan St; Category 2; Tel: 02372/52 03

Die Losieshuis
Probably the oldest hotel in Matjiesfontein. Children are very welcome and the restaurant rules are quite relaxed.
8 rooms; Logan St; Category 3; Tel: 02372/52 03

ENTERTAINMENT

Laird's Arms
Enjoy a beer in this Victorian pub.
Logan St

SURROUNDING AREA

Karoo (B-C 4-5)
This region covers 395200 sq km – about one third of the total area of South Africa. It has been described by geologists as one of the wonders of the world. Fossils uncovered here date back 240 million years. For those unfamiliar with desert landscapes, a tour through this vast and tranquil expanse of parched land is a fascinating experience. At dusk the sun disappears in a symphony of bright orange and red. The nights are cool, clear and perfect for star-gazing.

PORT ELIZABETH

(**D 6**) Although the British built a fort here in 1799, the first settlers didn't arrive until 1820. Port Elizabeth, or P.E. as it is usually called, was named after the wife of the city's founder, Sir Rufane Donkin. She had died in India at the age of 28, two years before his arrival in South Africa. The original settlement has now grown into a great city – the fifth-largest in South Africa (pop. 500 000). Initially, it was an important port and became known as the 'Liverpool of the Cape Colony'. Several European car manufacturers now have factories here, making it the centre of the South African motor industry.

Recently, the city has developed into a major tourist destination. Its golden beaches extend for over 16 km along Algoa Bay and like much of the surrounding area, it enjoys long, hot summer days and balmy tropical nights.

SIGHTS

Apple Express

This steam locomotive, once used to transport fruit, chugs its way along a narrow-gauge track, 283 km in length, from Port Elizabeth through the fruit orchards to Loerie in Long Kloof. ⭐ The view from the Van Staden River bridge is magnificent.
Every second weekend in the month; Humewood Road Station; tickets must be booked in advance; Tel: 041/507 23 33

Campanile

⭐ This tower marks the spot where the first British settlers came ashore. It is 53 m high and affords a fine view over the city.
At the entrance to the docks; the 23 bells in the bell-tower ring daily at 8.22, 13.32 and 18.02; Mon, Tues, Thurs-Sat 09.00-13.00 and 14.00-16.00, Wed 08.00-12.30

Donkin Reserve

When Sir Rufane Donkin was laying the foundations for Port Elizabeth in 1820, he declared that this open space was to be left as parkland. The stone pyramid beside the lighthouse is a memorial to Donkin's beloved wife.
Belmont St

Snake Park

The Snake Park, which is part of Port Elizabeth's *Oceanarium*, has more than 1000 snakes. They are periodically 'milked' of their poison which is used in the production of anti-venom serums. Other attractions include daily dolphin and sea-lion performances, marine aquariums, the *Tropical House* which houses birds and reptiles, and the *Night House*. This is lit with artificial moonlight that confuses the nocturnal animals into thinking day is night so that visitors can observe them awake.
Daily 09.00-13.00 and 14.00-17.00, dolphin performances at 11.00 and 15.00; Humewood Beach

MUSEUMS

Humerail Museum

You can enjoy a ride to King's Beach on the *Dias Express* steam train. The narrow-gauge railway starts at the Campanile and the train ticket includes a visit to the railway museum. As well as seeing some old railway locomotives and coaches, visitors are also welcome to watch the fitters at work

Port Elizabeth: centre of the motor industry and a popular holiday destination

in the workshops where rolling stock is repaired.
Mon-Fri 07.30-16.00, Sat/Sun 10.00-16.00; Humewood Rd

Local History Museum
Occupying one of P.E.'s oldest houses (1827), this museum keeps a collection of early 19th-century furniture. Other displays include an exhibition of dolls.
Sun/Mon 14.00-17.00, Tues-Sat 10.00-13.00 and 14.00-17.00; 7 Castle Hill

RESTAURANTS

De Kelder
As in all the holiday resorts, fish restaurants abound here. De Kelder is well known for the quality of its seafood.
Promenade; Category 2; Tel: 041/ 53 27 50

St George's
Enjoy a full meal or just a cup of tea in the green surroundings of the St George's Park restaurant.
Category 3; Tel: 041/52 26 02

SHOPPING

Greenacres and the *Bridge Shopping Centre* in Cape Road are South Africa's largest shopping malls.

HOTELS

Edward Hotel
The Edward is situated in the old town by the Donkin Reserve- and offers a fine view over the harbour and the city.
116 rooms; Belmont Terrace; Category 3; Tel 041/56 20 56, Fax 56 49 25

Walmer Gardens Hotel
Close to the airport, this small hotel is set in beautiful grounds.
27 rooms; 10th Avenue; Category 3; Tel/Fax: 041/51 43 22

SPORT & LEISURE

Diving
Divers are drawn here by the shipwrecks which lie on the sea bed off Port Elizabeth.
Information from Ocean Divers International; Tel: 041/55 27 23

Deep-sea fishing
For information on deep-sea fishing excursions, contact *Owen Charsley, Tel: 041/55 30 89*.

Windsurfing
Windsurfers can be hired on most of the beaches.

INFORMATION

Tourist Information
Donkin Lighthouse Building; Tel: 041/52 13 15

SURROUNDING AREA

Addo Elephant Park (D 6)
More than 200 African elephants thrive in this 9000-hectare nature reserve, 72 km north of Port Elizabeth. During the 1920s, they were nearly wiped out, but under the watchful eye of the park rangers, the elephants have been encouraged to breed and their future is now secure (*open daily all year round, gates close at 18.30*). Close by, on the banks of the Bushman River, the *Shamwari Game Reserve* offers anyone who does not wish to travel up to the game reserves of the northern provinces the opportunity to see the 'big five' – buffalo, elephants, leopards, lions and rhinos.
30 rooms; Summersand; Category 1; Tel: 042/851 11 96, Fax: 851 12 24

Diaz Cross (D 6)
A replica of the cross that Bartholomeu Diaz erected in Kwaaihoek in 1488.
Kwaaihoek, near Beknes Beach

**Mountain Zebra
National Park** (D 5)
This nature reserve on the northern slopes of the Bankberg hills was set up in 1937 to prevent the extinction of the mountain zebra, the smallest and very rare species of zebra. The project was a success; in 1964 there were only 25 left while today they number around 200. Other animals which thrive in the safety of the reserve are wildebeest, eland, springbok, birds and reptiles. There are hiking trails throughout the park and overnight accommodation in chalets is available.
Tel: 0481/24 27 and 012/343 19 91

St Francis Bay (D 6)
❀ ⚘ ⚓ St Francis Bay, Cape St Francis, Paradise Beach and Aston Bay are all popular holiday resorts overlooking the wide bay west of Port Elizabeth. There is no better place to look for shellfish than along these lonely beaches. St Francis Bay lies at the mouth of the Kromme River. If you follow the river upstream for 12 km, you will soon discover that this region is very popular with anglers. Holiday homes line many of the canals around the mouth of the river and surfers from all over South Africa and beyond converge on the beach which was once the venue for the world surfing championships. *Cape St Francis Holiday Resort (Category 2; Tel: 0423/94 04 20)* is situated by the beach.

STELLENBOSCH

(B 6) ★ Stellenbosch is South Africa's second-oldest town (pop. 42 000). Simon van der Stel, the governor of Cape Town, went on many expeditions into the interior and he was so struck by the beauty of the valley that in 1679 he decided to found a settlement there. From a stroll along the oak-lined streets, it is easy to imagine how Stellenbosch may have looked in its early years. The heart of the old town centre has been faithfully restored. The grand, Gothic-style *Moederkerk* church dates from 1863 and the town centre is dominated by a square with a large grassy open space known as the *Braak*, formerly used as a parade ground. The streets around the square are lined with Stellenbosch's prettiest and oldest houses. The University of Stellenbosch, which acquired its status in 1918, is the oldest university in South Africa and is centred around *Victoria College* (1886), one of the country's finest buildings.

The mountainous area surrounding Stellenbosch is known as Boland and is a major wine-producing area of South Africa. The fertile valleys are cultivated with vineyards and dotted with Cape Dutch homesteads many of which offer food and wine tasting.

SIGHTS

Bergkelder
Many fine South African wines are produced here.
Guided tour through the wine cellars and sampling Mon-Sat at 10.00 and 15.00; Tel: 021/887 24 40

Dorp Street
The tree-lined main street is the oldest street in the town and many of the buildings along it are listed. Most date from the 19th century. The Lutheran church, which was built in 1851, now houses the university art gallery. Even some of the oak trees in this street are protected by a conservation order.

MUSEUMS

Stellenryck Wine Museum
In addition to documenting the history of wine-making with some interesting exhibits of old tools and equipment, this museum also features a fine collection of Cape Dutch furniture.
Mon-Sat 09.00-12.45 and 14.00-17.00; Sun 14.30-17.30; Dorp St

Village Museum
Four restored houses, each dating from a different period, make up this museum which illustrates how the townsfolk of Stellenbosch lived between 1709 and 1850. The *Schreuder House* was built in 1709 by the German Sebastian Schröder and is the oldest town house in South Africa. *Bletterman House*, the local judge's residence which was built in 1789, is furnished in late 18th-century style. The neo-classical double-storey *Grosvenor House* has an interior décor in keeping with the styles that prevailed during the first decades of the 19th century. *Bergh House* was the home of Marthinus Bergh who lived here with his family in the 1850s and 60s. Even the gardens have been laid out as they would have been at the time.
Mon-Sat 09.00-17.00, Sun 14.00-17.00; Ryneveld St

RESTAURANT

Die Volkskombuis
In a house designed by the eminent architect, Herbert Baker, this restaurant serves traditional Cape cuisine in a comfortable and authentic atmosphere.
Wagenweg; Category 3; Tel: 021/887 21 21

Oom Samie Se Winkel
Typical 19th-century village shop.
84 Dorp St

D'Ouwe Werf
Traditional hotel.
25 rooms; Church St; Category 3; Tel: 021/887 16 08, Fax: 887 46 26

Lancerac Hotel
Outside the town, nestling in the grounds of a splendid vineyard.
30 rooms; Tel: 021/887 11 32, Fax: 887 23 10

Oude Libertas Centre
In summer, this open-air theatre stages operas, ballets and plays. Spectators can bring their own picnic baskets.
Dec-April; Adam Tas Rd; Tel: 021/808 74 74

Stellenbosch Publicity Association
De Witthuis, 30 Plein St; Tel: 021/883 35 84

Meerlust (A-B 6)
This vineyard, which is situated between Cape Town and Stellenbosch, has been owned by the Myburgh family for eight generations and the estate buildings rank among the finest examples of Cape Dutch architecture. Meerlust is best known for its red wines as well as its brandies. The estate is open to the public, but you should call first to book an appointment.
Tel: 021/843 35 87

Stellenbosch Wine Route (B 6)
❀ Over 20 wine estates within a 12-mile radius of Stellenbosch have opened their doors to tourists, offering wine-tastings and meals. The picturesque wine route, which winds its way through rolling vienyards, is clearly signposted. A map of the wine route is also available. For further information, contact the *Stellenbosch Wine Route Office, 30 Plein St. Open daily 09.00-17.00.* If you would like a guide to show you the way, then get in touch with *Vineyard Ventures, Tel: 021/434 88 88, Fax: 434 99 99.*

Take a wine-tasting tour of the vineyards around Stellenbosch

The heartland

Idyllic walks, wildlife parks and acres of farmland

The landlocked Orange Free State is bordered by the Northern Provinces, KwaZulu/Natal and the Cape Provinces. The State was founded by Boers who had set out on the Great Trek northwards, believing they had finally escaped from English rule. Winberg, the oldest town in the province, was founded in 1835. In its early years it was also the province's capital. The little town owes its name not to a battle victory, but to a dispute over land ownership won by a Boer who subsequently called his farmstead Wenburg or 'Won Castle'. Surrounded by vast plains and large maize and cereal farms, Winburg is still typical of the rural towns in the Orange Free State.

Freedom from the British interference was not to last long. In 1846, British officers arrived, bought the Bloemfontein farm and converted it into a military base. The settlement expanded to become the largest town in the

Lesotho, the 'Kingdom in the Sky', is an independent state within South Africa

Orange Free State. Once again, the Boers took to their wagons, trekked off and crossed the Vaal River into Transvaal. Six years later, the British, tired of the constant territorial disputes, gave up their claims to the land and agreed to the establishment of an independent free state. However, with the discovery of diamonds on the Orange River, they wanted to reclaim power over the valuable territory. Violent confrontations ensued between the Boers, the British and the local tribes, as people flocked here from all over the world. Twenty years after it had been declared independent, the Orange Free State once again fell under British rule and became part of Cape Colony.

The province stands on a plateau, which is largely flat and covered with endless fields and grassland, although it is not without its contrasts. In the east are some spectacular mountain ranges with snow-capped summits in winter. The uplands route that runs between Harrismith in the north-east and Zastron in the south provides the best

MARCO POLO SELECTION: ORANGE FREE STATE

1 Lesotho
Independent kingdom within South Africa (page 66)

2 Hamilton Park, Bloemfontein
The largest orchid collection in South Africa (page 65)

3 Golden Gate Highlands National Park
Named after the impressive sandstone cliffs which shimmer like gold in the scorching sun (page 66)

opportunity to enjoy the beauty of this region. It winds its way through spectacular scenery and passes some ancient rock paintings made by prehistoric inhabitants. Bethlehem owes its name to the pious Boers who were so impressed by the landscape that they decided to name the town after Jesus' birthplace and its river after the biblical Jordan river.

Nestling close to the foot of the Maluti Mountains, the Golden Gate Highlands National Park boasts some spectacular sandstone rock formations and a wide range of wildlife. Qwa Qwa is hidden away high up in the mountains. Lying at an altitude of about 2000 m, this region was created in the early 1980s as a homeland for southern Sotho people. An impoverished area, it is nevertheless surrounded by impressive mountain peaks and gently rolling hills. Sotho handicrafts are renowned throughout the country, especially the handwoven woollen carpets.

The town of Riemland in the north-east of the Orange Free State, was founded by the early Boer settlers who slaughtered the huge herds of game that grazed these open plains. They sold their hides which they cut into narrow, strips (*riem*). A painting in one of Cape Town's art galleries entitled *The Greatest Hunting Expedition of the Century* portrays the animal culls that took place throughout the province. In 1860, a hunt was held near Bloemfontein in honour of Prince Alfred, Queen Victoria's son – 4000 antelopes were shot dead in just one day.

As well as the National Park, there are also many game farms, which breed animals such as the springbok, South Africa's national emblem. These farms can usually be identified by their high fences, which run alongside the roads to stop the agile creatures from bounding into the road.

The heart of the province is occupied by the *Goldfields*, an area about 50 km in length and 16 km wide. More than one third of South African gold is mined in this region. First traces of the precious metal were discovered around 1903. Prospecting began about 30 years later, but early attempts to find reserves of any significant quantity were not successful and the pioneers gave up, having incurred great losses. After World War II, the Anglo-American Corporation invested millions of dollars in drilling and geological investigations. This region has been at the centre of the mining industry ever since. The new gold-mining town of Welkom, laid out in 1947 in a grid formation, is the second largest town in the Orange Free State. A number of its mines can be visited by appointment.

BLOEMFONTEIN

(**D 4**) Bloemfontein is the capital of the Orange Free State (pop. 190 000) and the seat of South Africa's Supreme Court. The history of the town goes back to 1840, when a *Voortrekker* by the name of Johannes Brits built a farm here. He named the settlement after a nearby spring (*fontein*) that was surrounded by flowers (*bloemen*). The British soon followed, buying up the land and establishing a military base here. The settlement developed into a town which, for many decades, was a melting pot for Boer and British influences. Frequently referred to as the 'City of Roses', Bloemfontein, with its many fine parks and gardens, still lives up to its name.

First Raadzaal
The oldest building in Bloemfontein was built in 1849. Its thatched roof was the work of Major Warden, who took charge of the first British soldiers in the region. This house was, in turn, centre of the local government, church and a school.
Mon-Fri 10.15-15.00, Sat/Sun 14.00-17.00; St Georges St

Fontein
A pillar marks the spot where the spring, after which the city was named, once flowed.
Selbourne Ave

Hamilton Park
★ One of the city's many old parks, situated at the bottom of Naval Hill. The greenhouse here is home to South Africa's largest

Bloemfontein: capital of the Orange Free State

Bloemfontein: a melting pot of Boer and British influences

collection of orchids. Temperature and irrigation for the 3000 plants are computer-controlled.
Mon-Fri 10.00-16.00, Sat/Sun 10.00-17.00; Union Ave

National Museum
A superb collection of fossils (including a dinosaur) accompanies a clearly laid out and thorough exhibition on the history of the Orange Free State.
Mon-Sat 09.00-16.30, Sun 14.00-17.00; Aliwal St

De Oude Kraal
A lovingly restored farmstead converted into a hotel about 35 km outside Bloemfontein.
8 rooms; the Riversford exit off the N1; Category 3; Tel: 05215/636, Fax: 635

Gliding
The upland plateau around Bloemfontein is popular with gliders from around the world.
Tel: 051/405 84 89

Bloemfontein Information Office
Hoffmann Sq; Tel: 051 40 54 89

Golden Gate Highlands National Park (E 4)
★ ◁ ▷ This nature reserve is named after two spectacular sandstone cliffs that loom up on either side of the road like a gateway to the area, and shimmer like gold in the evening sunlight. The 6000-hectare grounds provide a habitat for many native species including eagles which nest in the high crags of the Maluti Mountains. There are two camps in the park which offer overnight accommodation in huts.
On the A49 between Bethlehem and Harrismith; Tel: 012/343 19 91

Kroonstad (D 3)
This attractive town in the north of the Orange Free State on the banks of the Vals River, was founded by *Voortrekkers* in 1855. It is named after the trek leader's favourite horse, Kroon. Probably the most impressive aspect of the town is its fine array of old trees.

Lesotho (E 4)
★ ◁ ▷ An independent state in the heart of South Africa. Situated high up in the mountains, it is often referred to as the Kingdom in the Clouds. About the size of Belgium, Lesotho is the home of the Basotho tribe who settled here at the beginning of the 19th century. The capital, Maseru has a number of good hotels, such as the *Maseru Sun*, *(200 rooms; Category 1)* with the adjoining *Cabanas casino*. Maseru

makes a good base for excursions into the surrounding countryside. Street market traders sell a variety of handicrafts made of straw, such as the traditional pointed hats (*mokorotlo*). The hand-spun mohair wool is of excellent quality.

Thaba Nchu (E 4)

Founded in 1873, this small town is now an administrative centre and trading post for the Tswana tribe. Situated at the foot of the Thaba Nchu Mountain, it has a number of historic buildings and churches which are worth a visit. The nearby *Thaba Nchu Sun* is a top-class hotel located in a nature reserve. In the evening, guests can try their luck at the casino.
300 rooms; Category 1; Tel: 011/780 50 00

Welkom (D 3)

The town was laid out according to plans drawn up by the chairman of the Anglo-American Corporation, Sir Ernest Oppenheimer. It is divided into residential, industrial and mining districts, which are linked together by green, open spaces to form a harmonious whole. No road junction is controlled by traffic lights; all the interchanges are roundabouts. The smaller communities of Virginia and Odendaalsrus share Welkom's many facilities, which include an airport, hotels, restaurants, a car racing track, sports grounds, a theatre complex and even a local radio station.

If you want to visit one of the gold mines, you'll need to book one of the day-long tours in advance through the *Welkom Publicity Association, Tel: 057/352 92 44.* Traditional dance performances are part of the package.

Welkom is also a birdwatcher's paradise. Lakes in the surrounding area provide natural habitats for large flocks of flamingos and many other bird species.

Lesotho, home of the Basotho tribe

Home of the Zulus

This eastern province on the shores of the Indian Ocean offers travellers plenty of variety

The impressive KwaZulu/Natal landscape is both beautiful and varied. Although the province is relatively small, it offers holiday-makers a host of different opportunities for an enjoyable vacation: from the African bushland in the north to the wide east coast beaches lapped by the Indian Ocean. The climate is sub-tropical and the green, hilly landscape criss-crossed by rivers. But the most spectacular area of all is the *Drakensberg*, considered by many to be one of the most beautiful mountain ranges in the world.

Strands of European, African and Asiatic cultures combine to create a fascinating mixture. The nine-million strong Zulu population are by far the largest ethnic group. From 1820 to 1880, a large part of Natal was the Kingdom of Zululand and descendants of the notorious warriors still inhabit the area. The reputation of this tribe and its legendary leaders Shaka and Dingaan has spread far beyond the kingdom's bound-

aries. In 1816, at the age of 29, Shaka became chief of the Zulus. He was the illegitimate son of the former king, but with a combination of brutal ambition and military brilliance, he worked his way to the top and left no-one in any doubt as to who was the new king. He built up an army of 60000 warriors, which he kept busy with military campaigns. Other tribal groups were violently defeated or surrendered to his might. Shaka trained his men to perfection and developed new weapons for them. The eastern boundary for his kingdom was the Tugela River. Even the first European settlers, British traders who arrived here from Cape Town, accepted this river as the boundary. Beyond it, they built a trade mission for passing ships.

In 1838 the first *Voortrekkers* arrived in Natal in their ox carts. In the meantime, Dingaan had murdered his brother Shaka and had inherited the leadership of the Zulu people. The Boers sent their leader, Piet Retief, to negotiate with the new chief about land and peaceful co-existence, but to no avail. The whole dele-

Zebras and impalas in the Hluhluwe Game Reserve

gation was murdered by Zulus, who then attacked the Boers' main camp, killing several hundred men. They burnt down Port Natal and the inhabitants were forced to flee, their only escape route was via the sea. The angry Boers took a terrifying revenge and decimated the Zulu armies at the famous Battle of Blood River. Following their victory, the white settlers declared the region the Republic of Natalia and made Pietermaritzburg the capital. But the dream of an independent country did not last long. In 1843 Natal was declared a British Crown Colony and most Boers packed up and moved on in desperation. The ensuing wars between the Zulus and the British led to the destruction of the once mighty Zulu kingdom. Many of the tribal traditions, however, have lived on and if you take a trip through Zululand today, you will still see the tribesman in their kraals living their life in much the same way they did centuries ago.

The climate is ideal for the cultivation of tropical plants and fruit. In the middle of the last century, settlers introduced sugarcane. The crops flourished and the huge plantations and estates are still very much in evidence. As slavery had been abolished and the Zulus did not wish to work in the fields, workers were shipped across from India. They originated from the lower castes of Indian society and, in most cases, were happy to have work.

The KwaZulu/Natal coast is a holiday paradise. There are many resorts with magnificent beaches north and south of Durban, the largest and most popular holiday destination. The region offers something for all tastes. You will find peace and quiet in the small villages and leisure facilities in the larger towns such as Margate and Umhlanga. The scenery around the Drakensberg Mountains is incredibly beautiful. Sometimes known as the South African Alps, this range extends from Eastern Cape to the north-east of the country. One of the highest peaks is the 3299 m-high *Mont aux Sources*. The 'Mountain of Beginnings' is the source of five rivers, including the Tugela River. A

MARCO POLO SELECTION: NATAL

1 Indian markets in Durban
A fascinating mix of Asian and African (page 72)

2 Valley of a Thousand Hills
The countless rolling hills of this valley offer breathtaking views of a beautiful region (page 74)

3 Umhlanga Rocks
A popular holiday resort by the Indian Ocean (page 74)

4 Eshowe
One of the oldest settlements in Zululand where the acclaimed television series *Shaka Zulu* was filmed; the set is now a hotel (page 73)

5 Drakensberg Mountains
The dramatic and challenging landscape of the 'South African Alps' attract walkers and mountain climbers from all over the world (page 75)

series of giant rocks form a natural amphitheatre some 8 km in length, part of the *Royal Natal National Parks* which boasts some superb landscapes, rare flowers and wildlife. It is just one of Natal's many parks devoted to plant and wildlife preservation. The *Umfolozi Game Reserve* was created to provide a sanctuary for the 'big five' – elephant, rhino, lion, leopard and buffalo. The *Mkuzi Game Reserve* on the lower reaches of the *Lebombo Mountains* was established in 1912. It too is teeming with wildlife. Alongside giraffes, black rhinos, zebras and hippopotamus, there are large herds of blue wildebeest, reedbuck and waterbuck.

DURBAN

(**F 4**) Thanks to its broad white beaches and 300 days of sunshine a year, Durban has developed into South Africa's most prominent resort. It's hard to imagine that less than 150 years ago the city and its busy port were nothing but a primeval forest where lions and elephants once roamed. The Zulus still refer to Durban as *Ethekwini* – the quiet town.

The Portuguese explorer, Vasco da Gama, was the first European to set eyes on this paradise on his way to Asia. He landed in the harbour on Christmas Day, and named the bay area Natal (Portuguese for Christmas). In 1835, it was renamed after the governor of the Cape Colony, Sir Benjamin D'Urban.

After Mexico City, Durban (pop. 1 100 000) is now the fastest growing city in the world. It is a fascinating mixture of Asian, African and European cultures.

Half of the inhabitants are descended from the Indians who were brought here by the British colonial masters to work on the sugar plantations. A large part of Durban's appeal lies in its colourful blend of Indian markets, mosques and shops. Now that apartheid is gone, the diversity of the city's culture is confidently showing its face.

SIGHTS

Aquarium and Dolphinarium
The main attraction of this ocean aquarium is the shark pool where you can observe sharks basking in the waters off Durban. Over a thousand different species of fish are kept in the various tanks – the biggest holds up to 820 000 litres of water. The dolphinarium next door features regular daily performances.
Daily 09.00-16.00 (last admission), shows at 10.00, 11.30, 14.00, 15.00 and 17.00; the fish are fed at 11.00 and 15.00; Corner of West Parade and Marine Parade

Harbour tours and boat trips
Durban's port is the largest and busiest in the country. More freight is loaded and unloaded here than at any other harbour in Africa. Sightseeing tours of the harbour and romantic trips out to sea depart from the Pleasure Cruise Terminal.
Sarie Marais Jetty; Tel: 031/305 40 22

Juma Mosque
This mosque is reputed to be the largest and the finest in the southern hemisphere. Definitely worth a visit.
Corner of Grey St and Queen St

Natal Shark Board

The waters along Natal's coastal strip are shark-infested and more than 300 nets have been stretched across the inshore waters to protect bathers. If you want to learn more about sharks, the research institute opens its doors to the public once a week.
Wed only 09.00-11.00 and 14.30; on a hill above Umhlanga

Rickshaws

Zulus in traditional costume offer rickshaw rides along the beachfront promenade.

Umgeni River Bird Park

Observe a wide variety of exotic birds from all over the world.
Open daily; Marine Parade across the Umgeni River bridge.

MUSEUMS

African Art Centre

Exhibition and sale of original Zulu arts and crafts.
Mon-Fri 09.00-17.00, Sat 09.00-13.00; 35 Guildhall Arcade

Local History Museum

The former courthouse has been converted into a museum with displays of clothes, furniture and other items of interest illustrating Durban's early history.
Mon-Sat 09.00-17.00, Sun 11.00-17.00; Aliwal St

RESTAURANTS

The Deck

Enjoy the view and the sea air just as you would if you were sitting on the deck of an ocean liner.
139 Lower Marine Parade; Category 3; Tel: 031/37 17 47

Sea Belle

The very best in Indian food, but a 20-km drive from Durban.
Sea Belle Hotel; 62 South Beach Rd; Category 3; Tel: 0322/410 48

Le St Geran

Regarded as one of the 10 best restaurants in South Africa.
Aliwal St; Category 1; Tel: 031/304 75 09

SHOPPING

Indian Market

★ ⚥ An absolute must. The 180 or so stalls set out along Victoria Street sell spices, fish and meat, fruit and vegetables, and a variety

Durban's thriving tourist industry is based around its long beach

of arts and crafts. The *Oriental Arcades* offer similar wares. Street traders deal in jewellery, silk, saris, etc. As in any other oriental market, haggling is par for the course.
Closed Sunday; Victoria St and Oriental Arcade between Crey Rd and Cathedral Rd

The Wheel
A four-storey shopping centre with shops, restaurants and bars.
Gillespie St

HOTELS

Holiday Inn Crown Plaza
Thoroughly recommended, and not just for its spectacular views over the Indian Ocean.
444 rooms; Snell Parade; Category 2; Tel: 031/37 13 21

The Royal
The top hotel in the city centre. An amalgamation of old colonial style and modern comforts.
272 rooms; 267 Smith St; Category 1; Tel: 031/304 03 31

SPORT & LEISURE

Surfing, windsurfing and sailing
Surfing: *Tel: 031/37 40 38*; Windsurfing: *Tel: 031/22 41 59*; Sailing: *Tel: 031/657 26*

Water Wonderland
For watersports enthusiasts.
Snell Parade; Tel: 031/32 97 76

Selborne Country Lodge
Formerly a country residence (c. 1880), Selborne Park is now a hotel surrounded by extensive grounds and an 18-hole golf course. 60 km from Durban.
16 rooms; Pennington; Category 1; Tel: 0323/975 11 33

ENTERTAINMENT

Golden Mile
The Golden Mile is one long stretch of back-to-back entertainment venues for holidaymakers that runs parallel to the beach for more than 6km. Hotels, restaurants, bars and night clubs supply most of the fun. The *Natal Playhouse* has five theatres staging a variety of productions that cater for all tastes, from cabaret to opera. Street vendors hawking everything from beaded jewellery to ostrich eggs add to the lively atmosphere.
Beach Promenade

INFORMATION

Durban Unlimited
160 Pine St; Tel: 031/304 49 34

SURROUNDING AREA

Dingaans Kraal (Umgungundlovu)   (F 4)
It was here that the Boer leader, Piet Retief, and his men were murdered by Zulu chief Dingaan in 1838. The kraal has been rebuilt and is now a museum in the midst of some spectacular scenery.
On the R34 towards Vryheid

Eshowe   (F 4)
★ Eshowe is one of the oldest settlements in Zululand. It is a charming place, not far from the coast, on the edge of the Zulu heartland. The TV series *Shaka Zulu*, based on the life and times of the legendary Zulu king, was shot in the area in a purpose-built village which was subsequently converted into a hotel complex (*Hotel Shakaland*; Category 2; Tel: 03546/912, Fax: 842).

Hluhluwe Game Reserve (F 3-4)

This wildlife park at the foot of the mountains presents a unique combination of landscapes. Misty mountain forests, thornveld, savannah and dense thickets provide a habitat for a wide variety of mammals, including black and white rhino, elephants, buffalo, zebras, lions and leopards. Lucky observers may catch a glimpse of a nyala, a spiral-horned antelope, one of Africa's most beautiful but elusive animals. ⬱ Visitors can be accommodated overnight in luxurious tree-houses linked by wooden walkways. The views from them are lovely (*Category 2; Tel: 035/562 01 44, Fax: 562 02 05*). Safaris in the three reserves of Hluhluwe, Umfolozi and Mkuzi can be arranged from here (*Tel: 0331/47 19 81, Fax: 47 19 80*). The *Zulu Museum* is open daily. Not far from Mkuzi is the *Phinda Tzilwane reserve.* The rangers here are trying to re-introduce lions and elephants (*42 rooms; Tel: 011/803 84 21, Fax: 803 18 10*).

Kwabulawayo (F 4)

Shaka's former capital is marked with a simple monument. At a nearby hotel you can sample the lifestyle of the old sugar barons (*Mine Own Country House; 5 rooms; Gingindhlovu; Category 3; Tel: 0353/ 30 12 62, Fax: 30 10 25*).

Valley of a Thousand Hills (F 4)

★ ⬱ The view from Botha Hill over the hills and valleys is quite spectacular. Early in the morning before the mist rises, you can sometimes hear the Zulu cries as they communicate to one another across the mountains. Some 500 m beneath the *Rob Roy Hotel* (*37 rooms; Category 3; Tel: 031/777

13 05, Fax: 777 13 64), lies a kraal, where you can watch Zulus performing tribal dances and witch doctors practising their craft.

Ulundi (F 4)

Ulundi (literally 'high place') lies in the heart of the old Zulu kingdom. The KwaZulu Cultural Museum here documents the history of the Zulu people (*Mon-Fri 08.00-16.00*). Accommodation is available in replica Zulu huts. Enquire in the museum. The only other hotel in the town is the *Holiday Inn Garden Court* (*62 rooms; Category 2; Tel: 011/482 35 00*).

Umhlanga Rocks (F 4)

★ A popular holiday destination by the Indian Ocean, with excellent places to bathe and good surfing conditions. The other main attraction is the crocodile farm *Croc World*. Tribal dances are held in the *Croc World Zulu Kraal* (*Wed and Sat; Tel: 0323/211 03*). There are a number of hotels overlooking the beach. One of the best is the *Oyster Box* where the oysters are much sought-after (*93 rooms; Category 2; Tel: 031/561 22 33, Fax: 561 40 72*).

PIETERMARITZBURG

(E4) Pietermaritzburg (pop. 170 000) lies in a broad valley surrounded by green hills. Although the old town with its fine Victorian houses reflects a predominantly British colonial influence, Pietermaritzburg was actually founded by the Boers, who settled here after the Battle of Blood River. They established the Republic of Natalia and named the capital after their two leaders, Piet Retief and Gerrit Maritz.

SIGHTS

Voortrekker House
The only surviving house from the pioneering days.
Mon-Fri 09.00-17.00, Sun 09.00-12.30; 333 Boom St

MUSEUMS

Macrorie House Museum
Houses an interesting collection of Victorian furniture that belonged to the early British settlers.
Tues, Wed, Thurs and Sun 11.00-16.00; corner of Pine St and Loop St

Voortrekker Museum
Former church now housing a collection of memorabilia.
Mon-Fri 09.00-13.00, 14.00-16.30, Sat 08.00-12.00; 340 Church St

RESTAURANT

White Mischief
One of Natal's best restaurants.
180 Loop St; Category 1; Tel: 0331/42 45 79

HOTELS

Imperial Hotel
This old Grand Hotel is the finest in town. It is named after Louis Napoleon, the French Imperial Crown Prince. He stayed here before joining the war against the Zulus in 1879, where he met an early death at the age of 23.
43 rooms; 224 Loop St; Category 2; Tel: 0331/42 65 51, Fax: 42 97 96

Rawdons Hotel
An idyllic spot in the tiny village of Nottingham Road.
37 rooms; Category 3; Tel: 0333/360 44

INFORMATION

Pietermaritzburg Publicity Association
177 Commercial Rd; Tel: 0331/45 13 48

SURROUNDING AREA

Drakensberg Mountains (E 4)
★ ☙ The Natal Drankensberg's main attraction is the 8-km long, 2000-m high amphitheatre in the *Royal Natal National Park* – an awesome sight. Numerous rock paintings, the work of Bushmen who sought shelter here, have been found in the area. In the *Giant's Castle Game Reserve*, there is a museum of Bushman drawings (*daily 11.30-14.30*). The reserve, which was originally established to provide sanctuary for the eland, is also one of the best places to observe birds of prey such as the Cape vulture, lanner falcon, snake eagle and the endangered bearded vulture. There are many hotels in the area; most have a view. Recommended are *Cathedral Peak Hotel (90 rooms; Category 3; Tel/Fax: 036/ 488 18 88)* and *Champagne Castle Hotel (49 rooms; Category 3; Tel: 036/468 10 63)*.

Howick Falls (E 4)
The Umgeni River plunges 111 m into a spectacular gorge below.
Umgeni Valley Nature Reserve by the road to Howick

Midmar Nature Reserve (E 4)
The Midmar Dam is a popular resort for watersports enthusiasts. The nearby *Midmar Historical Village* is an open-air museum illustrating life in Natal during the pioneering era (*currently open on Sun only; Tel: 0332/30 20 67*).

The land of gold and diamonds

Formerly the Transvaal, this mineral-rich region has been divided into the North-west, Gauteng, Eastern and Northern Transvaal

Your voyage of discovery begins the moment you land at Jan Smuts airport and step off the plane into the early African morning. The first impressions will not be disappointing as you breathe in the clear dry air from the uplands, and see before you expanses of land tinged with red, endless desert and the breathtakingly beautiful sunrise typical of the north of the country.

This was the last region to be settled by whites. The industrial metropolis of Johannesburg is just over 100 years old and neighbouring Pretoria only a few decades older. Wesel Pretorius, the founder of the capital, named the town after his father, one of the Boer generals at the Battle of Blood River. After the declaration of the free province of Transvaal in 1854, South Africa comprised two British colonies, the Cape and Natal, together with the Boer republics of the Orange Free State and the Transvaal. Once

The Three Rondavels by Blyde River Canyon in the Drakensberg Mountains of Eastern Transvaal

diamonds were discovered in Transvaal, the British tried to persuade the Boers to form a confederation. When this failed, the British annexed the republics, an action which triggered the first war between the British and the Boers. Afrikaners still refer to this battle as the *Vryheidsoorloog* or the War of Liberation. The Boers won and in 1881 Transvaal regained its independence. The country grew under the leadership of the legendary Paul Kruger. When, in 1886, gold reserves were discovered not far from Pretoria, he knew the influx of foreigners would cause problems, but it was not possible to keep the discovery a secret. In the ensuing gold rush thousands of people descended on the region.

After gold was discovered, the British were even more determined to re-integrate this part of southern Africa into the empire as a Crown Colony and the situation led in 1899 to the outbreak of the second Boer War. In 1902 the Boers conceded defeat and in 1910 the Republic of South Africa with Pretoria as its administrative capital was established.

The area where gold was discovered is known as Witwatersrand. It is a high plateau that rises to an average altitude of 1700 m. The seam of gold extends for over 130 km and is as wide as 30 km in places. Many mining and industrial towns, the largest being Johannesburg, are located in this region. The Vaal River is a popular weekend destination for Johannesburgers and there are many fine hotels in the area. Alternatively cabins and holiday homes are available for rent.

The university town of Potchefstroom, founded in 1838, was the first capital of the Boer Republic of the Transvaal. Although the capital was moved to Pretoria in 1860, the town has remained an important cultural centre and many of the original period buildings have survived.

The *Great North Road* begins just north of Pretoria. This route runs through hilly bushland to Warmbad (a spa town whose hot springs are used to treat rheumatism) and continues northwards for hundreds of kilometres via Waterberg and Pietersburg, through baobab country, across the Soutpansberg Mountains, before finally reaching the Limpopo River, which forms the border between South Africa and Zimbabwe (to the north) and Botswana (to the north-west). This journey to South Africa's northern frontier is highly recommended for those who really want to get to know the country.

Eastern Transvaal (Mpumalanga) is the best-known and most popular of the northern provinces. Another spectacular scenic road is the *Panorama Route* which runs along the edge of

The gold rush left its mark all over the country

South Africa's interior plateau with a dramatic descent to the sub-tropical plain below. Gold was discovered in this region long before the stampede to Witwatersrand began. *Pilgrim's Rest*, now a ghost town and tourist attraction, was an important settlement in the early gold rush. Some of the old mines are still working but, for a long time now, the cultivation of sub-tropical fruit has been the main source of income in these parts. The magnificent panoramas over the bizarre landscape and giant waterfalls are unforgettable. Even more enthralling is *Kruger Park*, one of the biggest and best game reserves in Africa. A number of private wildlife reserves have opened up along the western edge, where experienced rangers accompany tourists on safari. These guides are familiar with the ways of the animals and they can help newcomers to appreciate and enjoy the animals and plantlife.

JOHANNESBURG

(**E 3**) Situated at an altitude of 1753 m, Johannesburg enjoys more sunshine than California. The days are always warm, even in winter, although it can get very cold at night. It is by far the largest city in South Africa (pop. 1.9 million). If you include the population of the black suburb of Soweto, then the number of inhabitants within the greater Johannesburg conurbation rises to more than 4 million – not including all the other shanty towns in the outer suburbs.

When it comes to location, architecture and natural beauty, Johannesburg cannot compete with Cape Town. Nevertheless, it is an energetic town with a fascination all of its own. The atmosphere is hectic, the lifestyle fast and breathless though sometimes a little impersonal. This young city is the nation's commercial and financial centre; everything revolves around money and business. The Stock Exchange is here, as are the largest airport, the widest roads and the tallest skyscrapers. If you climb up to the viewing platform in the Carlton Centre and survey the city's glittering skyline, it soon becomes evident that this is the engine of the South African economy. The price of land and property in the inner city is so high that it pays to demolish older buildings and build upwards. In its short history, Johannesburg has been rebuilt three times, and still it continues to grow. It won't be long before it merges completely with Pretoria in the north.

Known to the black population as *E'Goli*, the city was quite literally 'built on gold'. It all began in 1886 when George Harrison, an Australian sculptor who had prospected for gold in his own country, was travelling through Eastern Transvaal where he recognized the distinctive appearance of gold-bearing rock. What followed has been recorded in history as the greatest gold rush of all time. Gold-diggers from three

MARCO POLO SELECTION: THE NORTHERN PROVINCES

continents set out on what was then a long and arduous journey into the southern African interior. It took just 100 years for the town to develop from a settlement of tented camps and wooden huts into the third biggest city in Africa, where gold is still a major source of prosperity.

SIGHTS

Carlton Panorama (K 11)
⚡ The 50-storey Carlton Centre skyscraper with its shopping mall, cinemas, exhibition space and viewing platform on the top floor is Johannesburg's most dominant landmark. The view extends over the city to the Magaliesburg Mountains.
Daily 09.00-23.00; Commissioner St

Gold mines (0)
Visits to gold mines can be arranged through the Chamber of Mines. As part of your tour you can watch how liquid gold is turned into bullion. To make the most of your visit, allow a whole day. Traditional dance performances are held at some mines on Sundays. Note that visitors under 16 and over 60 are not allowed underground at any time.
Tel: 011/838 82 11 for reservations

Gold Reef City (0)
★ The gold rush era is brought to life in this reconstruction of a gold-mining town. Among the faithfully reproduced buildings are houses, shops, saloon bars, a brewery, an apothecary, a Chinese laundry, a tailor and a newspaper office. Tours of the site can be made either on a narrow-gauge railway or in a horse-drawn carriage. You can also visit a disused

mine and follow the complete process from the extraction of the ore to the pouring of the molten gold into moulds. No. 14 shaft was once the world's richest gold-mine.
In the Crown district 15 minutes from the city centre; Horizon Tours coaches leave from Sandton Sun Hotel and the city-centre hotels; Tel: 011/496 16 00

Gold Reef City

Lion Park (0)
Watch the lions roaming freely from the safety of your car. Not for those of a nervous disposition.
Daily 08.00-17.00; 30 km from Johannesburg on the R512 towards Lanseria Airport

Soweto (0)
Short for South Western Townships this sprawling Johannesburg suburb came to prominence in 1976 when the bloody repression of a protest by school-children and the ensuing violent clashes horrified the world. Populated by 2-3 million blacks, most of whom live below the poverty line, Soweto is still a troubled area. Many do not approve of Soweto being part of a tourist itinerary. A difficult choice for the tourist, but if you do wish to visit it, go with a guide.

For information about guided tours, contact Jimmy's Face-to-Face Tours; Tel: 011/331 61 09

MUSEUM

Africana and Geological Museum (I 10-11)
The Africana section focuses on the history of the city and colonization of the country. The geological section has a big display of minerals and a unique collection of gold and gold-bearing rock.
Mon-Sat 09.00-17.30, Sun 14.00-17.30; Corner of Sauer St and President St

Johannesburg Art Gallery (K 9)
An international collection of works by South African artists.
Tues-Sun 10.00-17.00; Joubert Park

Museum Africa (H 10)
Exhibition on the life and culture of the peoples of South Africa – from the Stone Age to apartheid.
Tues-Thurs 09.00-17.00; Bree St

RESTAURANTS

Casalinga (0)
Near Rocky Ridge Golf Course some way from the city centre, but worth the journey.
Category 1; Tel: 011/957 26 12

Gramadoelas at the Market (H 10)
One of the few restaurants to offer the full range of South African fare.
Corner of Bree St and Wolhuter St; Category 2; Tel: 011/838 69 60

Zoo Lake (0)
〰 In the park by Zoo Lake with a fine view.
Jan Smuts Rd; Category 1; Tel: 011/ 646 29 91

HOTELS

Gold Reef City Hotel (0)
Comfortable hotel in reconstructed gold-mining town.
45 rooms; Alamein Rd; Category 1; Tel: 011/496 16 26, Fax: 496 16 36

Lesedi (0)
Lesedi is a Sotho word meaning 'place of light'. This traditional village offers visitors overnight accommodation.
On the R512 towards Lanseria, exit opposite the airport; Category 3; Tel: 01205/513 94, Fax: 514 33

Rosebank Hotel (0)
In a delightful part of the city with many shops and restaurants in the vicinity.
Chr. Tyrwhitt and Sturdee Ave; Category 2; Tel: 011/ 447 27 00

The Westcliff (H 7)
This Orient Express Hotel was opened at the beginning of 1997. Situated in one of Johannesburg's smartest suburbs.
64 rooms; 67 Jan Smuts Ave; Tel: 011/23 10 50, Fax: 23 10 60

SHOPPING

African Herbalist Shop (H 10)
★ For an alternative view on those niggling complaints try consulting a medicine man or woman.
14 Diagonal St

African Rooftop Market (0)
Over 450 stalls selling everything from jumble to antiques.
Sun 09.30-17.00; Rosebank Mall, 50 Bath Ave

Hyde Park Corner (0)
Small but smart shopping centre.
Hyde Park

Sandton City (0)

Johannesburg's largest and most impressive shopping centre. One shop after another selling everything you could ever wish for.
Sandton district

ENTERTAINMENT

Hard Rock Café (0)

Trendiest spot in town. The place to be seen.
Thrupps Centre, 204 Oxford Rd, Illvoho; Tel: 011/447 25 83

Market Theatre (H 10)

♣ ☯ South Africa's top productions are staged at the Market Theatre's four venues. The successful musical *Sarafina* was first performed here. A book shop, an art gallery, bar and restaurant occupy part of the refurbished Indian and citrus-fruit warehouse. The theatre complex itself is housed in the grandest of the market buildings. Built in 1911, it has a typical Beaux-Arts façade. Many alternative shops and galleries can be found in the vicinity.
Wolhuter St; Tel: 011/832 16 41

INFORMATION

Johannesburg Publicity Association (K 10)

Corner of Market St and Kruis St; Tel: 011/336 49 61

SURROUNDING AREA

Hartbeespoort Dam (E 3)

The reservoir that was formed by the Hartbeespoort dam lies between Johannesburg and Pretoria in the Magaliesburg Mountains. The lake reserve has crocodiles, aquatic birds and seals and is definitely worth a visit. There are reg-

ular balloon flights over the dam, weather permitting (*Tel: 01205/ 510 21*). A snake park and breeding centre for leopards, cheetahs and other rare animals have also been established in the vicinity.
Wild Cheetah Centre; Tel: 012/504 19 21

Sun City, a mega pleasure complex

Sun City and Lost City (D 2)

★ South Africa's entertainment mecca is a two-and-a-half hour drive from Johannesburg. Like an oasis in the desert, it emerges out of a dry and desolate bush landscape. The hotel and casino complex nestles in the tranquil surroundings of the Pilanesberg Mountain, an ancient volcanic crater. Night after night, busloads of gamblers and pleasure-seekers descend on Sun City's three hotel complexes in the hope of hitting the jackpot. *The Cascades*, *Sun City* and *Cabanas* offer every comfort. Each one has its own sports facilities and swimming pool, and the nearby lake has facilities for every conceivable kind of watersport. The 18-hole golf course was designed by South Africa's golfing hero, Gary Player. Parts of the park resemble a primeval forest yet everything is man-made. No waterfall, palm tree, flamingo or parrot ever existed here before Sun City was built. To see the real thing, you can go on safari in the nearby National Park. There is no shortage of choice for evening entertainment here: you can dine out in one of the elegant restaurants, have a flutter in the casino, play the gaming machines or take in a show.

In 1992, a fourth hotel complex was opened up on an adjacent 26-hectare site. The Lost City is a fantasy world. The fairytale *Palace* hotel is surrounded by an artificially created rainforest with waterfalls and lakes, and an artificial desert (complete with golf course). The idea behind its design was to recreate something of the lost worlds of Africa.

Sun City has its own station and an airport with daily flights to and from Johannesburg. The Sun City Express transports day-trippers from the car park to the main attractions. Daily bus connection from Johannesburg; Tel: 011/780 78 00 and 014651/21 00

Wonder Cave (E 3)

This cave with its incredible stalactites and stalagmites is over two thousand million years old. It is one of South Africa's most impressive natural phenomena.
Daily 08.00-17.00. Tours every 90 minutes from 08.00 onwards. Beyond Randburg on the R47.

PRETORIA

(E 3) When the South African parliament is not sitting in Cape Town, the nation is ruled from Pretoria (pop. 820 000). For half the year, government is seated in the Union Buildings. The imposing edifice, which stands on top

of a hill to the east of the city, was designed by Sir Herbert Baker in 1913, following the establishment of the South African Union in 1910. The huge amphitheatre can accommodate 2000 people. The parliament buildings are set in an impressive park, bordered by ministerial and embassy premises.

Johannesburg and Pretoria are completely different in character: one is vital and cosmopolitan, the other peaceful and staid. While Johannesburg is an urban jungle, Pretoria is full of parks and gardens. The city is seen at its best in October when the 70 000 jacaranda trees which line 500 km of the city's streets are in bloom, and the pavements are bathed in a delicate shade of lilac.

SIGHTS

National Zoological Garden
✔ With its 3500 different species, this zoo is one of the largest in the world. A cable-car transports visitors above the enclosures to strategic viewing points.
Daily 08.00-18.00; Paul Kruger St

Union Buildings
★ The seat of government is situated on top of the Meintjieskop hill. It is considered by many to be one of the masterpieces of South African architecture. It was on the steps of this building that Nelson Mandela was sworn in as president of the new multi-racial South Africa.

Voortrekker Monument
This massive granite monument was erected in memory of those who died in the Battle of Blood River. It symbolizes the courage and indomitable spirit of the

The Union Buildings, where the South African parliament meets for half the year, dominate the city

trekkers. In the Hall of Heroes, a series of 27 marble reliefs illustrates the story of the Great Trek. *Mon-Sat 09.00-16.45, Sun 11.00-16.45; Fontains Valley*

MUSEUM

Transvaal Museum
This museum houses an interesting collection of geological and archaeological finds, including the remains of prehistoric ape-men. *Mon-Sat 09.00-17.00, Sun 11.00-17.00; Paul Kruger St*

RESTAURANTS

Chagall's
Good food and relaxed atmosphere. Set in lovely grounds. *Fontains Valley; Category 1; Tel: 012/341 75 11*

La Madeleine
After many years, this is still Pretoria's number one restaurant. *Esselen St; Category 1; Tel: 012/44 60 76*

Oeka Toeka
Offers traditional Afrikaans food in a Victorian setting. *Kotze St; Category 3; Tel: 012/341 00 84*

SHOPPING

Bushman Shop
A good place to pick up some original souvenirs. *Central St*

HOTELS

Mount Grace
One of the finest country hotels in the area. *65 rooms; Magaliesburg; Category 2; Tel: 0142/77 13 50*

Victoria Hotél
The Rovos Rail Group spared no expense in restoring this turn-of-the century hotel to its former glory. *28 rooms; corner of Scheiding St and Paul Kruger St; Category 1; Tel: 012/323 60 52, Fax: 012/323 08 43*

Pretoria Publicity Association
On the corner of Walt St and Vermeulen St; Tel: 012/313 79 80

Crocodile River Arts and Crafts Ramble (E 3)
Head first to the Magaliesburg Mountains and then carry on in the direction of Honeydew. Several well-known African artists have their studios along this route and they sell their work from their homes during the first weekend of every month.

Cullinan Mine (E 3)
It was here in 1905 that Thomas Cullinan found the world's largest diamond. The 3106-carat 'Cullinan' was presented to King Edward VII by the Transvaal government in 1908.
Guided tours Tues-Fri 09.30 and 11.00, no access to children under 10; Premier Diamond Mine, Cullinan, via the R513; Tel: 01213/400 81

Kruger National Park (F 2)
★ The world-famous 2-million-hectare wildlife park is home to Africa's widest range of species. Of the eight entrances to the park, four can be reached from *Nelspruit*: *Malelane, Crocodile Bridge, Numbi* and the *Paul Kruger Gate. Orpen* and *Phalabora Gate* are roughly in the middle, while *Punda Maria* and *Pafuri* are on the north side. A range of accommodation is offered, from well-equipped cottages to huts. The smaller camps are self-catering, while the larger ones, such as the *Pretoriuskop* and *Berg-en-Dahl*, have their own restaurants and swimming pools.

South Africa was one of the first countries to recognize the importance of animal conservation. At the end of the last century, President Kruger agreed to the establishment of the Sabie Game Reserve between the Sabie and Crocodile rivers as the game populations were diminishing rapidly. The area was later extended into what is now the Kruger National Park. This magnificent reserve provides habitats for 130 species of mammal, 48 species of fish, 114 reptile and 468 bird species. The reserve contains some 8000 elephants, 26 000 buffaloes, 120 000 impalas as well as zebras, leopards, cheetahs, giraffes, rhinos and much more.

The park has a network of good roads and visitors can drive through at their leisure observing the animals. A speed limit of 50 km/h applies on the asphalt roads, 40 km/h on the tracks. It is important not to exceed these limits, not only to avoid a heavy fine, but also to avoid frightening the animals away. The best times to see game are early in the morning, before 10.00, or in the evening on an organized night safari.
Oct-Mar 05.30-18.00, April-Sept 06.00-17.30; Information and reservations: National Parks Board; Category 3; Tel: 012/343 19 91, Fax: 343 20 00

Mala Mala/Rattray, Londolozi and Sabi Sabi Game Reserve (F 2)
A number of private game reserves are situated at the western edge of the Kruger National Park. The animals that are protected within these reserves are no different from those in the Kruger Park, but the areas are

much smaller. The accommodation offered to visitors, however, is more luxurious and more expensive. You are more likely to see the 'big five' – lions, elephants, buffalo, rhinos and leopards – on a guided jeep safari as the game wardens who conduct them know where the animals are likely to be.

Night safaris are offered by the private reserves. During the day, when the sun is at its hottest, most creatures find a shady spot and take it easy, while at night, the animal kingdom comes alive.

Mala Mala/Rattray Reserve is the largest and oldest private game reserve in South Africa. Some 18 000 hectares in area, it shares 30 km of its border with the Kruger National Park. Accommodation, food and the safaris are all first class. For guests who wish to go on hiking safaris, 'Trekker Trails' offer overnight accommodation in luxury tents (*there are several camps offering accommodation at varying prices, but all are Category 1; Tel: 01311/656 61 or 011/789 26 77, Fax: 886 43 82*).

Londolozi Game Reserve is not quite so luxurious, but far from cheap. Accommodation is available in three camps along the Sand River.

◁▷ *The Tree Camp* is built around an old ebony tree and offers a magnificent panorama (*Category 1; Tel: 011/784 70 77, Fax: 784 76 67*).

Sabi Sabi Game Reserve also borders the Kruger National Park and its guests here are accompanied by rangers. In the evening, delicious grilled game is served under a starry African sky (*Category 1; Tel: 011/ 483 39 39, Fax: 483 37 99*).

Eastern Transvaal (F 2)

A predominantly sub-tropical region of great beauty. If you come here via the ◁▷ *Panorama Route*, you will be greeted with magnificent views over the forests and plains. When gold was discovered in Barberton near the Swaziland border, the area was invaded with prospectors. The settlement expanded rapidly as rich gold deposits were unearthed in the surrounding hills but the reserves were quickly exhausted. It is now a sleepy, but attractive little town.

Sabie (F 2)

A pretty little town surrounded by thick forests. The main attractions in the vicinity are: the *Mac-Mac* falls (14 km); Pilgrim's Rest, a well-preserved gold-mining town, from the turn of the century; and the scenic Mount Sheba National Park (*Mount Sheba Hotel; 25 rooms; Category 2; Tel: 013/768 12 41, Fax: 768 12 48*).

Tzaneen (E 2)

★ This colourful town by the banks of the Letaba River nestles at the foot of the Drakensberg Mountains. The name *Tzaneen* is a Hottentot word meaning 'in a basket' – the basket being the beautiful valley in which the town lies. The local economy is based on timber, cotton and tropical fruit. ◁▷ *World View* is a spectacular vantage point with a sweeping view of the Letaba valley and the Drakensberg Mountains. About 15 km south of Tzaneen in *Agatha* is *The Coach House*, one of South Africa's top hotels. It offers pure, undiluted luxury in a superb environment (*45 rooms; Old Coach Rd; Category 1; Tel: 0152/307 36 41, Fax: 307 14 66*).

Practical information

*Important addresses and other useful information
for your visit to South Africa*

BANKS

There are no restrictions on the amount of foreign currency you can carry with you, but visitors are not permitted to take more than 500 rand into or out of the country. Some banks accept Eurocheques, but traveller's cheques are a safer bet. All the major credit cards are widely accepted.
Bank opening times: Mon-Fri 09.00-15.30, Sat 08.30-11.00

BARS

The main bars of some hotels are not open to women, though most hotels have a 'Ladies Bar'. Many bars in the rural areas do not serve alcohol on Sundays, unless it is with a meal.

BED & BREAKFAST

Private accommodation at very reasonable prices can be found throughout the country. Bed and breakfast guest houses are popular as they provide foreign visitors with the opportunity to meet some of the local people.
Central reservation, Tel: 011/880 34 14, Fax: 788 48 02

CAMPING

Given the climate, South Africa is an ideal place for camping holidays. All the towns have good campsites and there are plenty of well-equipped sites in and around the beach resorts, in the wildlife parks and game reserves. Most have swimming pools, shops and restaurants. Caravans and camper vans are accommodated.
For further information, Tel: 011/789 32 02

CAR HIRE

The cost of car hire in South Africa is generally quite reasonable. The main car hire firms have offices in all the big towns and most of them offer special rates for tourists:
Avis Tel: 08000/211 11
Budget Tel: 08000/166 22
Imperial/Hertz Tel: 08002/102 27
Those on a tighter budget may wish to hire a car through *Rent a Wreck, Tel: 011/402 70 43*. Its prices are much more competitive than the multinationals and although the vehicles are not exactly in mint condition, they are nowhere near as bad as they sound.

Before you set out, however, make sure you are clear about what to do in the event of a breakdown.

The minimum age requirement is 23 and drivers must have an international licence.

COMPUTICKET

Computicket is a central reservation system for cinemas, operas, plays and other events. You will find Computicket offices in the department stores and shopping malls of most main towns.

CUSTOMS

The duty-free allowances for adults are as follows: 400 cigarettes, 250 g tobacco, 1 l spirits, 2 l wine, 50 ml perfume, 250 ml eau de toilette and gifts to the maximum value of R200.

DRIVING

All drivers in South Africa are obliged by law to take out third party insurance to cover personal injury, but comprehensive cover is advisable. The speed limits are 60 km/h in built-up areas, 100 km/h on trunk roads, 120 km/h on motorways. The road network between the main cities and outlying towns is very good. Some 84 000 km of South Africa's roads are surfaced, while a further 163 000 km are just dirt tracks.

Driving is on the left. Do not drive if you have been drinking alcohol. Drink-driving is a serious offence and the authorities come down heavily on offenders. South Africa has one of the world's worst driving records, so be vigilant. Seat belts are compulsory and traffic laws are strictly enforced.

Bourke's Luck Potholes on the Panorama Route

The police will only attend an accident if injuries have been sustained. In all other cases, drivers should exchange addresses and report the accident at a police station. It is not essential to carry your driving licence at all times. Should you be required to present it, you will normally be given 24 hours to take it to the nearest police station.

The Automobile Association of South Africa breakdown service covers the whole of South Africa. *Tel: 011/403 57 00*

EMBASSIES/CONSULATES

Diplomatic Offices abroad

United Kingdom:
South African High Commission Trafalgar Square, WC2N 5DP Tel: 0171/930 4488

Republic of Ireland:
South African Embassy Heritage House 23 St Stephen's Green, Dublin 2 Tel: 01/661 5553

United States:
3051 Massachusetts Ave, NW
Washington DC 20008
Tel: 202/232 4400

Foreign embassies in South Africa
United Kingdom:
Greystoke, 255 Hill St
Arcadia, Pretoria 0083
Tel: 012 433 121

Republic of Ireland:
Tulbagh Park, 1st floor, Delheim suite,
1234 Church St, Colbyn, Pretoria
Tel: 012/342 5062

United States:
Broadway Industry centre, 4th floor
Heerengracht Foreshore, Cape Town
Tel: 021/214 280

GOLF

Enquiries: *Golf Union, Johannes-*
burg, Tel: 011/640 37 14

HOTELS

All the main hotel chains such as
Protea, Southern Sun, Holiday Inn
and Sun International offer special
tourist deals (see also p 33).

INFORMATION

South African Tourism Board
United Kingdom and Ireland:
5/6 Alt Grove, Wimbledon
London, SW19 4DZ
Tel: 0181/944 8080
Fax: 0181/944 6705

United States:
500 Fifth Ave, 20th Floor, suite 2040
New York NY 10110
Tel: 212/730 2929

Details of local information centres
are given throughout this guide.

INOCULATIONS

Visitors to the Kruger National
Park and the nearby game reserves will need to protect themselves against malaria, before,
during and after their stay.
Consult your local GP for information on inoculations and recommended medication. It is
inadvisable to swim in rivers and
lakes in the eastern and northern
regions of the country as the
bilharzia parasite may be present.

If you are travelling to South
Africa from a yellow fever zone,
you will have to produce a
certificate of inoculation.

MEDICAL CARE

South Africa does not have a
national health service. Medical
treatment must be paid for by
the patient, so it is essential that
you take out travel insurance
which covers accident, illness
and hospitalization. Doctors are
listed in the telephone directory
under Medical.

PHOTOGRAPHY

Military installations, police
stations and prisons may not be
photographed.

PERSONAL SAFETY & EMERGENCIES

Police/emergency services: 10111
You should be safe on your visit
as long as you take certain basic
precautions. Always lock your car
from the inside when travelling
in towns. Never walk through
the inner city at night and keep
your wallet and camera well
out of sight. It is recommended to
keep valuables in the hotel safe.

The Table Mountain cable-car goes right to the top

POST & TELEPHONE

With the exception of a few rural areas, the South African telephone network is fully automated and you can dial direct almost worldwide. Calls abroad from pay-phones will require a lot of coins. Many post offices provide an international phone service. Mobile phones can be hired at the airport.

International dialling codes:
UK: 09 44
Ireland: 09 353
USA: 09 1
Dialling codes in South Africa:
South Africa country code – 27
Cape Town – 021
Durban – 031
Johannesburg – 011
Pretoria – 012
Directory enquiries: 10 25
International directory enquiries: 10 23

Normal post office opening hours are: *Mon-Fri 08.00-16.30 and Sat 08.00-12.00.* Some of the larger offices have extended opening hours. Stamps can only be bought from post offices.

RIVER RAFTING

River rafting trips are organized on the Tugela, Orange River and Vaal River and they last from one to six days. Special deals are offered to families and beginners. For further information contact *River & Safaris, Tel: 011/803 9775, Fax: 803 96 03.*

SAFARIS

A wide range of safari tours are available to suit all tastes and pockets. For further information contact *SATSA (Southern Africa Tourism & Safari Ass.); Tel: 011/883 91 03, Fax: 883 90 02.*

Top recommendation: *Lindbergh Lodge*, about three hours' drive from Johannesburg. Cecil Rhodes was just one of the celebrities who stayed the night in this elegant country house when it belonged to the Lindbergh family. The game reserve in which the Lodge is situated is comparable to the Serengeti. The park keepers organize a variety of different tours, including balloon safaris; drifting above the grazing wildebeest, giraffes, kudus and zebras is a truly unforgettable experience. (*15 rooms; Wolmaranstad; Categories 1 and 2; Tel: 01811/220 41, Fax: 220 48*).

TIME

South African Standard Time is two hours ahead of Greenwich Mean Time throughout the year.

TRAIN TRAVEL

The majority of rail services across South Africa are slow and uncomfortable, but there are two notable exceptions: the *Blue Train* and *Rovos Rail*. The leisurely journey on either of these luxury trains is highly recommended.

The Blue Train runs from Cape Town to Pretoria, with a stop in Johannesburg, and the journey takes about 24 hours. Smoothly and noiselessly, but still relatively slowly, the train leaves the green coastal region behind and heads north. The narrow-gauge track winds its way through fertile farmland and runs right across the Karoo in a straight line. It passes through the diamond fields and then on across the high northern plateau. During the journey, travellers can relax in the lounge, enjoy a meal in the smart restaurant car or stay in their compartment. The food is good and the wine list excellent. Compartments range from a rather cramped one-person cabin to large luxury suites complete with bathroom and lounge. The service is top-notch. You even get a bar of chocolate on your pillow. The Blue Train and its predeces-

sors have been running since 1901. Fares range from R950 for a single journey in a single cabin to R8130 for a return journey in a luxury suite. *Reservations in Johannesburg, Tel: 011/774 44 69.*

The golden age of the steam locomotive and luxury rail travel lives on in the lavishly restored Rovos Line which operates a number of different routes across the country and beyond. Eight 1920s carriages are hauled by three vintage locomotives, dating from 1893, 1926 and 1938. The owners spent many years locating and renovating carriages and engines. No more than 40 people – serviced by a staff of 14 – can travel on any one train. The food, which is served in a restaurant car that was built in 1924, is excellent. All the rolling stock, including the observation car, is furnished in turn-of-the-century style, but installed with all the modern conveniences you would expect. One of Rovos Rail's most romantic routes is a steam-hauled safari along the 1000-km stretch from Pretoria through Eastern Transvaal to Graskop. On this memorable journey passengers are transported back to the days of the great adventurers, fearless pioneers, gold-diggers and elephant hunters.

Rovos Rail also travels to Cape Town, the Victoria Falls and along the Garden Route. Once a year, the company organizes a 10-day journey to Dar-es-Salaam in Tanzania. The fare for trips within South Africa range from R2000 to R6000. *For reservations, Tel: 012/323 60 52, Fax: 323 08 43.*

Both journeys are very popular and bookings must be made a few months in advance.

VAT

VAT paid on goods over R250 can be reclaimed at Johannesburg, Cape Town or Durban airport. You will need the receipt as well as the form completed by the shop assistant which states your name and address, description and cost of goods, and the VAT paid. Queues at the refund desk can be long, however, so leave plenty of time. Goods sent directly to your home address are not subject to VAT.

For further information, Tel: 011/484 75 30, Fax: 484 29 52

VISAS

Visitors from the UK, Ireland and the US do not require a visa, but their passport must be valid for at least six months beyond the intended date of departure.

VOLTAGE

The standard voltage throughout the country is 220V. Plugs have three round pins – adaptors for European and American appliances can be bought from local hardware stores. Many of the larger hotels can supply adaptors.

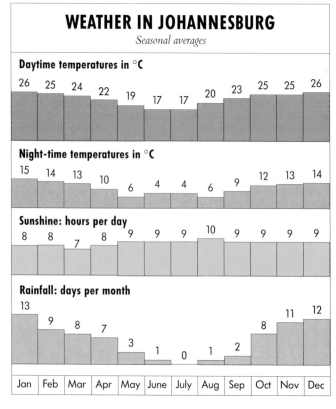

WEATHER IN JOHANNESBURG
Seasonal averages

Daytime temperatures in °C

Jan	Feb	Mar	Apr	May	June	July	Aug	Sep	Oct	Nov	Dec
26	25	24	22	19	17	17	20	23	25	25	26

Night-time temperatures in °C

Jan	Feb	Mar	Apr	May	June	July	Aug	Sep	Oct	Nov	Dec
15	14	13	10	6	4	4	6	9	12	13	14

Sunshine: hours per day

Jan	Feb	Mar	Apr	May	June	July	Aug	Sep	Oct	Nov	Dec
8	8	7	8	9	9	9	10	9	9	9	9

Rainfall: days per month

Jan	Feb	Mar	Apr	May	June	July	Aug	Sep	Oct	Nov	Dec
13	9	8	7	3	1	0	1	2	8	11	12

Do's and don'ts

*How to avoid some of the traps and pitfalls
the unwary traveller may face*

Beggars

Compared with other African countries, South Africa has relatively few beggars. At traffic lights or in car parks in the main cities, however, drivers are often approached by groups of children hoping for some spare change. Even though the sight of them can be quite heart-rending, it is better not to encourage the practice. These children are usually members of organized groups whose adult leaders quickly relieve them of any money they are given. If you wish to give something, keep some sweets or apples handy in the glove compartment. When driving through cities, it is advisable to keep your car door locked.

Feeding animals

Feeding animals in the wildlife parks is strictly forbidden, and that includes the baboons that congregate by the roadside and around wayside stopping places. Many of them have lost their natural timidity towards human beings and while you may be charmed by their curiosity, you should keep your wits about you.

They will often clamber on to the roof of a parked car, wait until the door opens, then jump inside and start rummaging for things to eat, grabbing hold of anything that is lying about. It is not unheard of for hand-bags full of passports and money to be snatched and carried off into the wilds.

Hitch-hiking

Given the unregulated public transport system, hitch-hiking is common. South Africans are usually very helpful and no-one ever has to wait too long for a lift to come along. Tourists should think twice, however, before picking up hitch-hikers. While you may wish to be helpful, it can be dangerous unless you are sure you are in a safe district.

Motorways

People's attitude to traffic may seem rather cavalier to motorists used to driving on the motorways of Europe. Don't be surprised to see people and dogs lined up on the hard shoulder waiting to cross, and watch out for cyclists and joggers, especially near the townships. Horses, cows and sheep, which are left to graze on the grassy strip beside the carriageway present another hazard.

Walking at night

When you are out at night in the big cities you should take sensible precautions. A stroll around the block after your evening meal, for example, is not really recommended. It is dangerous to walk through the dark, empty streets

Feeding the animals in the game reserves is strictly forbidden

of downtown Johannesburg at night. If your hotel is within walking distance from wherever you happen to be, go back along main routes and walk at a determined pace or, preferably, take a taxi. The same applies in the other big cities, notably Cape Town and Durban, although the beachfront promenades are usually quite safe to walk along. If you go up Table Mountain and want to find an isolated viewpoint away from the road, do not take any valuables with you. As in any country suffering from high unemployment and poverty, crime levels in South Africa are high, but if you act with common sense, it is unlikely that anything will happen to you.

Zebra crossings

When crossing the road in South Africa, and Cape Town in particular, do not expect motorists to stop automatically at pedestrian crossings. Similarly, motorists should not assume that pedestrians will always wait when the green light shows. Whatever the traffic lights may indicate, the locals expect motorists to stop.

The Cullinan Diamond

On 26 January 1905, the most magnificent diamond of all time was discovered in the Premier mine on the Witwatersrand, near Pretoria. It was named after Thomas Cullinan, a prospector of Irish descent who owned the mine. It weighed an incredible 3106 carats, was 100 mm long, 63 mm high and 51 mm wide. It was impossible to cut such a huge stone into a single gem, so it was divided into 9 diamonds of varying size and shape. The two largest diamonds, the pear-shaped Cullinan I (530 carat) and the cushion-shaped Cullinan II (317 carat), were presented to King Edward VII. Cullinan I, which the king called the 'Great Star of Africa', was set in the British Royal Sceptre where it remains to this day.

INDEX

This index lists the main places, sights and hotels mentioned in this guide.
Main entries are shown in bold, illustrations in italics.

What do you get for your money?

The South African unit of currency is the rand, which is divided into 100 cents. Coins come in denominations of 1, 2, 5, 10, 20 and 50 cents, and 1, 2 and 5 rand; there are notes of 5, 10, 20, 50, 100, 200 and 500 rand. Inflation is high in South Africa, but foreign tourists tend to benefit from the constantly fluctuating exchange rate. It is advisable, however, to change your pounds into rand in South Africa.

In most respects, South Africa is a cheap holiday destination for Europeans. For example, petrol costs half what you would pay back home, even though South Africa is not an oil-producing country. Cigarettes are also cheap. Admission to museums is often free; if there is an entrance fee, then it is very low and does not usually apply to children. A cinema ticket costs under £3. A pizza in a restaurant in Sea Point, a popular holiday resort near Cape Town, costs about £6, but you could buy a three-course meal in a country hotel for about the same price. A bottle of good table wine costs about £1.50 in a shop.

The major international credit cards (Visa, American Express, Mastercard, Diner's Club etc.) are accepted in most hotels, shops and restaurants in and around the big towns and main tourist areas.

£	Rand	Rand	£
1	7.67	1	0.13
2	15.34	5	0.65
3	23.01	10	1.30
4	30.68	15	1.96
5	38.35	20	2.61
10	76.70	30	3.91
20	153.40	40	5.22
30	230.10	50	6.52
40	306.80	60	7.82
50	383.50	70	9.13
60	460.20	80	10.43
70	536.90	90	11.73
80	613.60	100	13.04
90	690.30	250	32.59
100	767.00	500	65.19
200	1534.00	750	97.78
250	1917.50	1000	130.38
500	3835.00	5000	651.89
750	5752.50	7500	977.84
1000	7670.00	10000	1303.78

The conversion table above is based on the Thomas Cook tourist rate, October 97